THESE

OLD

BASTARDS...

by RENOIR

THESE OLD BASTARDS
Copyright © 2016 Renoir
All rights reserved.
ISBN: 978-0-9946174-0-8
Published by Meredian Pictures & Words 2016
Angels Beach, Australia
No parts of this publication may be reproduced, stored in a retrieval system, or transmitted in any form or by any means, electronic, mechanical, photocopying, recording, or otherwise, without the prior written permission of the copyright owner.
This book is sold subject to the condition that it shall not, by way of trade or otherwise, be lent, resold, hired out, or otherwise circulated without the publisher's prior consent in any form of binding or cover other than that in which it is published and without a similar condition including this condition being imposed on the subsequent purchaser. Under no circumstances may any part of this book be photocopied for resale.
Some names and identifying details have been changed to protect the privacy of individuals.

DEDICATION

For my late wife Gill,

who inspired the name of Gill's Old Bastards,

and inspired a whole lot more

and for Meredith

who continues to inspire me.

FOREWORD

G'day.

Thanks for buying this book. If you're reading it without buying, then do us a favour and stump up the cash – it's for a good cause.

The cause is *Gill's Old Bastards*, or G*O*Bs – the Brisbane branch of the Australasian Order Of Old Bastards. I'll tell you more about the AOOB in a bit, but what's important here is that all the profits from the sale of this book will go to charity. Charities that fight cancer, and that help sick kids.

G*O*Bs take our name from my late wife Gill, who lost her fight with cancer in 2006. (It's pronounced Jill by the way, so we're jobs, not 'gobs'.) Her passing was the spur for a few of us to get together to try to make a positive difference in our community. We've adopted the motto 'For Good Times, And Doing Some Good'.

The membership of G*O*Bs keeps growing, but I really want to thank Colleen, Gav, and most especially PK, who are right at the heart of making those Good things happen.

The stuff in this book comes from all over the place. A lot of it is stuff that's happened to me, or near enough for me to see. A lot of the stories came to me first hand from the people involved. A few are from the 'it happened to the friend of a friend' category but I reckon they're worth repeating anyway. I can't put my hand on my heart and swear it's all 100% true, but I'm not claiming to write history either.

A fair chunk of the stuff in this book came out a few years back under the title "*A Bunch Of Old Bastards*". I've tweaked some of that, added more bits, and tried to give you a bit more value for your book-buying buck.

The book is dedicated firstly to Gill. But it couldn't have happened without a bunch of other old bastards either – whether they knew they were contributing or not. A bloody big 'thank you' to all of them!

A special 'thank you' goes to Meredith, who's embraced and supported G*O*Bs with willingness and enthusiasm that inspire and delight me. I've been astonishingly lucky to be married to two such wonderful women – no, I don't understand it either, but I'm grateful!

Renoir

CONTENTS

WHO ARE THESE OLD BASTARDS, ANYWAY? 9

THE OLD BASTARD AT WORK I 11

THE OLD BASTARD AT PLAY 30

OLD BASTARDS ARE PEOPLE, TOO 57

THE BASTARD HAS A DRINK 80

THE OLD BASTARD ON THE ROAD 84

SOME DIFFICULT OLD BASTARDS 105

THE BASTARD'S NOT WELL 118

THE OLD BASTARD AT WORK II 122

NO BASTARD IN PARTICULAR 143

THE LAST WORD 152

MEMBERSHIP APPLICATION 155

WHO ARE THESE OLD BASTARDS, ANYWAY?

There was this war, see? There'd already been The War To End All Wars, but then another one came along, so they called it World War 2.

In the course of this bloody great unpleasantness a bunch of American servicemen got posted to Australia. It didn't always work out well – I'm not going to talk about the Battle Of Brisbane - but there was good stuff came out of the whole mess.

One or two of those visitors were particularly struck by the fact that in Australia "G'day ya old bastard!" was an expression of mateship, not the precursor to a fight. When they got back 'stateside' they kicked off something called the International Order Of Old Bastards.

Fast forward twenty or so years to 1968. In the British Lion Hotel, Glebe, a bloke named Leo Bradshaw and some mates kick off the Australasian Order Of Old Bastards. Leo and his mates were determined to raise as much money as possible for Camperdown's Royal Alexandra Hospital For Children, and the AOOB was to be their way of doing it.

The name caused a few problems. It was (and still is) a bit hard to convince some people to take seriously a charitable organization that so clearly doesn't take itself too seriously. But they stuck to their guns, and in 1973 the AOOB was officially recognized and registered as a charity.

New branches and new charities have come along. Camperdown Children's is now Westmead, but is still important to the AOOB. At last count the hospital had received around $1.5 million from the Old Bastards. All up, as of May 2016 a shade under seven million dollars has been raised and donated. Not bad, eh?

I first discovered the AOOB through Sam Weller's book *'Old Bastards I Have Met'*. Besides telling the story of the Order, Sam's book was a collection of yarns, stories and reminiscences. Sam was one of those blokes who'd have a go at just about any job, from cane cutting to flogging insurance to pouring beers and plenty in between. He'd seen and done plenty, and I reckon the book was a hugely entertaining read. Not only that, it won me over on the good work the AOOB does.

'Old Bastards I Have Met' came out in 1979. I don't reckon Sam's with us any longer, but if I'm wrong I'll be more than happy to shout the Old Bastard an

afternoon of ales in apology! I might not have quite the same pedigree as Sam, but I've been and done and seen a fair bit in my time too, and I reckon there are plenty of stories to be told of the last thirty-odd years.

Old Bastards may be young or old, male or female. I've met lazy OBs, cunning OBs, drunken OBs and, happily, a lot of funny Old Bastards. We've shared laughs and stories in a variety of places and circumstances. I'll tell some of them in the coming pages.

There's only one type of OB I really don't like, and that's the humourless old bastard. You know the type: miserable sods whose face you'd reckon would break if they tried to laugh. Sometimes they use the scourge called 'political correctness' as an excuse while they glare daggers and complain at anyone else having so much as a chuckle. Lucky there's not too many of them around. And they're not likely to be reading this anyway – so you and I can enjoy a few yarns, and sod 'em if they can't take a joke!

.o0o.

THE OLD BASTARD AT WORK I

Back when I was at high school, and in the early days of Uni, supermarkets were the great employers of my age group, fast food restaurants being nowhere near as common as they soon would be.

There was a very clear divide between jobs for boys and jobs for girls. The girls got to handle money and cash registers – the legendary 'checkout chicks'. Us blokes got to pack the big brown paper bags that groceries went in before plastic became the rage. Long before the eco-friendly green bags you get to pack for yourself now.

It's a funny thing. When the plastics started replacing the old brownies we were told it was because they were stronger and safer for the customer who was less likely to lose their groceries due to 'bag failure'. It didn't take long for cost cutting to mean most of the plastic bags were so flimsy they'd only hold a couple of decent-sized items before bursting, so you'd need a dozen bags to carry the fortnight's shopping.

Then we were told all these bags were an environmental hazard if we didn't dispose of them properly, and we should be paying extra for the privilege of using them, or else buying the environmentally friendly bags everyone's now offering. Perhaps we should have just stuck with the paper? Recycled paper even?

Stuffing groceries into paper bags wasn't often challenging work for most of us, so to alleviate the boredom some (young) old bastards would devise different ways to amuse themselves.

If a customer was particularly surly or rude to the checkout girl (especially if she was someone the packer fancied) then there were a number of evil fates that may befall their groceries. The simplest and most obvious thing was to pack the most fragile items at the bottom of the bag, with heavy stuff on top. Jostled around in the boot of a car, a half dozen eggs weren't likely to stand up too well to a half dozen big tins of dog food.

Mick was an old bastard in a store where I worked for a while, and he had a variation on this all his own. I reckon he must have had ideas of being a circus strongman or a pro wrestler. While a surly customer was facing the other way arguing about the price of a tin of sardines or suchlike, he would take a packet of SAO biscuits between the palms of his hands, and squeeze.

The idea was to crush the crackers and compress the packet as much as he could, then pull it back out to its usual dimensions and pack it, seemingly as normal.

Mick's greatest cracker crush came the day a customer was giving a really, really hard time to Eve the checkout girl. Eve had been Mick's unrequited love for some time, and while he'd never had the nerve to tell her he fancied her, you could see his temper go up a notch every time this shrill customer berated Eve for picking up groceries too roughly, or too quickly, or too slowly.

Unfortunately for the customer, her packet of SAOs came through the checkout fairly late in the order, by which time Mick was fairly steaming. While she was busy haranguing Eve over the price of beans, Mick did his strongman act.

I was watching from the next checkout as he ground the whole packet down to the thickness of a single biscuit, then carefully eased it back out to its usual shape. With great delicacy he placed it at the top of a bag of groceries and laid a couple of other items around it to preserve it. When the irate customer got home her mood would not have been improved by opening a packet of what could only have been SAO dust.

*

Besides packing groceries for customers, the other regular task for blokes in supermarkets was shelf stacking. This was supposed to be the work of the 'night fill' staff, but sometimes a delivery would arrive late, or there'd be a run on a particular item and we'd have to fill a shelf from the warehouse stock 'out the back'.

One day my old mate Smokey was working on stacking boxes of cereal. Now, Smokey was a likeable old bastard, with a quick wit and a terrific sense of humour. Trouble was, once he started to laugh he couldn't find the Off switch.

This particular day he was standing on a three step ladder, arranging on the top shelf the packets that were the 'reserves' for those closer to floor level. A little old lady came tottering along the aisle, clearly trying to find some particular item.

She spotted Smokey, and presumably reasoned that because he was on a ladder, he must be high up in the store. Or at least had a better view. Either way, he'd be the man to help her.

She gave the leg of his trousers a sharp tug, almost overbalancing him. "Excuse me, young man," she said. "Do you have crushed nuts?"

Smokey immediately started to crack up. Without thinking he replied, "No ma'am, I always look like this."

That finished him. He toppled off the steps onto the cereal packets, giggling hysterically, while the bemused little old lady went off to complain about 'the lunatic in aisle nine'.

*

There were some blokes who were never let loose in jobs where they might encounter a customer. Maybe they had a language problem so people couldn't understand them – that used to mean something once, in days when 'customer service' wasn't just a phrase in a management text book. Or maybe, like Wayne The Box, they just weren't bright enough to be seen representing 'the firm'.

Wayne was a nice enough Old Bastard, but not the sharpest knife in the drawer. In fact, most spoons would have an edge on him. But he meant well, was good at doing what he was told, and considering he wasn't real big, surprisingly strong.

That was how he got his nickname. Seeing him manhandle crates of tinned fruit like they were nothing a new bloke in the store remarked, "Jeez – he's as strong as an ox!"
Two of the older hands watching were less kindly disposed.
"The ox would be smarter," remarked one.
"The box of peaches would be smarter," added the other. And the name stuck.

Like a lot of blokes of that nature, Wayne never seemed to mind much what he was called. Just give him a job to do, leave him alone to do it, and pay him at the end of the week – he'd be happy. Nobody expected Wayne to deal with customers. His place was 'out the back' in the storeroom, shifting stuff and generally keeping the place tidy with whatever odd jobs the duty manager might give him.

Mind you, it was important to explain the job clearly. I remember when a fairly new boss Mario casually said "Wayne, clean the big freezer please." The 'big freezer' was a walk-in cold room where all the frozen food was kept before it went out into the store.

Normally, cleaning it was an easy job that involved checking for and removing empty or near-empty boxes, then giving the floor a quick sweep out. By chance, it was a task nobody had ever thought to give Wayne before. He'd cleaned the rest of the storeroom plenty of times though, and he figured he knew the drill.

A while later Mario noticed Wayne The Box running his hands under the warm water at the sink in the washroom, still shivering despite being rugged up in the thick parka kept for staff working in the 'big freezer'.

"Bloody cold in there, boss," observed Wayne before adding "Shelves are finished – just got the floor to do."

Mario gave him an odd look, but left it at "Okay – don't take too long," before going off to supervise some other task.

It was probably an hour later. Wayne had gone off on smoko, and Mario went to check on the job he'd done. I happened to be nearby watching when he donned the parka, opened the cold room door, took two steps inside and with a fearful yell disappeared from view. He'd slipped and skidded on his backside the entire length of the freezer. Wayne had cleaned it out like he did any other storeroom – with a mop and bucket.

The floor was covered by a quarter inch thick sheet of ice. Wayne must have started at the far end and worked back to the door, so was never at risk himself.

The only reason Mario hadn't had a big box of frozen peas come down on his head when he crashed into the wall at the end of his skid was that, thanks to Wayne, the peas weren't going anywhere. Like the floor, he'd cleaned the shelves the way he always did: with a wet cloth. Every box he'd lifted and put back down was frozen in place. No wonder the poor sod had been thawing his hands in the washroom!

*

Looking for a decent coat, I was pottering about in a good menswear store a while back. This very stuffy bloke came in and demanded to see the tailor. From out the back emerged the boss – a laconic old bastard who I reckon must have learned his trade during, or just after, World War 2.

The customer explained loudly that he's an Elder in his church and wanted to be fitted for a good new suit, made to measure, for "an important wedding".

"Righto," said the cutter, "It'll be ready in three weeks."

"That's not good enough!" raged the Elder. "The wedding is in less than a fortnight. You'll have to do better than that! The good Lord was able to make the world in only six days!"

The tailor just nodded and said, "Yep, and look at the state *it's* in."

*

Sometimes service staff mean well, or at least you hope so. Of course, they may equally well be having a subtle dig.

I was spending some time at Tallebudgera on the Gold Coast. Over breakfast I was watching a couple of American tourists who were clearly frustrated by Aboriginal place names.

I must admit, I've had trouble suppressing a few chuckles at some pronunciations of jaw-breaking names. Trouble is, when you live near them or hear them all the time you forget how daunting words like Woolloongabba, Cullacabardee or Numurkah can look when read for the first time. It's like driving in Wales through the likes of Pontrhydfendigaid and Cwmsychbant, or being confronted with Sgurr A'Gheadaidh or Camastianavaig on the Isle of Skye.

The tourist couple approached a waitress in the fast food joint where I was reading the paper.

"Hey girlie!" began the man in the loud shirt, "I wanna know where we are – an' say it real slow, huh?"

The young lady, who I suspect didn't consider herself a 'girlie', replied with great clarity and care "Mac. Don. Alds."

*

Nev told me about a waiter in a Greek restaurant he knew. Nev had gone out to dinner there with his wife. It was no special occasion, just a night off from the kitchen for both of them.

"I think I'll have the calamari," announced Nev's wife.

The waiter nodded. "Very good, madam. Would you like an entrée sized serve, or a main meal?"

"What's the difference?" she asked.

The waiter shrugged. "None, actually. The entrée just comes out sooner."

*

I don't want to say too much about used car salesmen. They have an unfortunate reputation for dishonesty that I've been told is quite unfair and undeserved. I've been told this by several people, all of whom were trying to sell me a used car, and in at least some of their cases I'm sure it's true.

The one thing I will share is a piece of advice I heard given to a new salesman by the car yard owner.

"Never admit that we haven't got what the customer I looking for. If they want a bright blue VW, you tell them 'I'm not sure if we have any in right now', then you lead them around the *entire lot*, looking. If they haven't already stopped to check anything out by the end you say something like 'well gee – if we had a blue VW I'm sure it'd be right around here. Sorry, one of the other salesmen must have beaten me to it. Did you happen to see anything else you like along the way?' And then you start moving them to the cars we *want* them to buy."

No lies were told in recounting this story.

*

Snowy used to be the Health & Safety Officer in a mining town out back. It's not a job that endears you to everyone around you. Management would rather not spend money on improvements or lose time when production gets held up while those improvements are made.

And the people doing the actual work usually would prefer to be left alone to get on with their jobs without interference – they reckon they know what they're doing and don't need an 'outsider' telling them to do anything differently.

Snowy came up with a novel way of endearing himself to everyone on the mine site. He quietly let it be known that there was something different about the soft drink machine in the canteen. If anyone paid their dollar fifty and pressed the bottom button when they came off their shift, instead of a can of cola they'd get a beer.

It did wonders for morale apparently. No one abused the situation, so the bosses didn't complain. And Snowy was the most popular Health & Safety Officer the town had ever had.

*

I admit to being a bit nonplussed when I heard about the latest In Thing in hair treatments to hit London. The fashionable and wealthy are conditioning their coiffures with "protein rich bull's semen".

I found that concept bad enough, but then it occurred to me: who collects the raw material? And I wonder what they put as 'Occupation' on their tax return?

*

One of the most aggressive bits of marketing that I've seen was a big sign that gleefully advised "Only 2 minutes drive to McDonalds!"

That might not seem too provocative until you consider the sign's location. It was on the side of a bus shelter, right by the driveway into a Hungry Jack's outlet.

*

I reckon that the people who design ads are sometimes a bit too close to their work to see it like their audience will. Take for instance a billboard I saw recently promoting Barrier Reef holidays.

There's a stretch of greenery and white sand away in the distance, but most of the picture is of a couple of people snorkeling in a big expanse of clear sunlit water. All a very attractive image, I must say – especially on a chilly winter morning.

The catch phrase emblazoned across the billboard was "Where life's mysteries become clearer". The problem is that the words are in white on a pale blue background, so they're not easy to read. To compound that, the very casual style of lettering they've used has the 'c' and 'l' of the last word very close together.

So at first sight the message appears to be "Where life's mysteries become dearer".

Mind you, I've heard some stories about the pricing practices adopted on small Barrier Reef islands that are owned and operated under monopoly arrangements. Once you're on *their* island you pay *their* prices for food and drink because you've nowhere else to go unless you happen to have a pretty decent boat of your own handy. Maybe 'dearer' is the right word after all.

*

I love how little changes in spelling can produce subtle or not so subtle changes in meaning. I went to a little restaurant that advertised the house "clear skin wines".

I wonder whether you were supposed to drink them, or rub them into troublesome complexions.

Similarly, I remember noticing a beachside snack bar in Fiji that advertised "sand witches". I suppose they were probably of the conventional ham, cheese and tomato type, but I did wonder whether there was some old island ritual magic involved in their making.

*

With the passing of time, the appropriateness of a name can change. Sometimes it's because the meaning or at least the popular usage of a word evolves. You don't see an ice cream called a Golden Gaytime being advertised much any more. It's still sold, but the ad campaigns seem to be too much for anyone to undertake.

Other times it's just that the reason behind the name loses currency. There's an excellent pub in the main street of the lovely little English town of Bourton-On-The-Water. It was a modern state-of-the-art building when it was constructed in 1712, and was proudly christened The New Inn.

More than three hundred years later it's still a fine building, but sometime along the way an owner has realized that the name was no longer appropriate. Now the pub's signage proudly welcomes you to The Old New Inn.

*

In a large American city I happened upon a shop selling a wide range of religious bits and pieces. All of the stock pertained to the Christian religion. While there were a few nice, understated or even elegant items, a large percentage could fairly be described as tacky.

Some of the items that caught my eye included a mouse mat depicting the Last Supper, a build-it-yourself balsa wood Nativity scene, and a range of velvet prints of the Virgin Mary.

Perhaps most disconcerting of all was a framed picture of Jesus which was printed on that funky plastic material that gives the illusion of movement when viewed from slightly different angles. As you moved around the shop the image of Jesus appeared to nod and wave His hand toward you.

I guess I shouldn't be surprised in the country that gave us Disneyland. This emporium of eye-watering icons was enthusiastically emblazoned "Holyland".

*

The owners of many hairdressing salons seem to have a fixation for puns that rivals my own. Some are funny (assuming you like puns), others don't just push the boundaries of good taste, they give them a right wallop.

I've seen variations on "Curl Up and Dye" and "A Cut Above" in towns and cities all over the world. Likewise "Hair Today, Gone Tomorrow" and "The Cutting Edge".

I don't imagine too many customers of Japanese origin were keen to visit "Hairishima". They may have been marginally more comfortable with "Hairi Kari".

Perhaps you might expect a religious experience at "Hairy Krishna". However "The Kindest Cut Of All" had no connection with any rabbinical services, as far as I'm aware.

Thinking of other services, the proprietors of "Blow" made sure there was no confusion as to the nature of their business by adding to their very prominent sign the words "It's A Hair Thing".

*

There are some quite basic instructions that new recruits to the armed forces get given that aren't in any of the manuals. They're good survival tips, though.

> Never go on a mission with anyone braver than you.
>
> If the enemy is within range then so are you.
>
> Never be the first to do something, and never be the last.
>
> Try to look unimportant out in the field. The enemy just might be low on ammunition.
>
> Look where you're going. Anyone can be a minesweeper. Once.
>
> Don't draw fire. It irritates the people around you.

In a similar vein to that last one is this advice from an Army 'preventative maintenance' manual: "A slipping gear could let your M203 grenade launcher fire when you least expect it. That could make you quite unpopular with whatever is left of your unit."

Some bastards have a gift for understatement.

Clearly, though, some of the people responsible for writing weapons manuals and instructions don't have a high regard for the intelligence of their audience. That itself is a cause for serious worry for the rest of us.

Take for example the instruction printed in large clear letters on a US Army rocket launcher: "Aim towards enemy".

*

On the subject of American weaponry, I wasn't sure whether to be impressed or appalled by a US Air Force officer I heard interviewed.

Questions were being asked about reports of American bombs accidentally landing on their own positions, or those of their allies. It had been suggested that there were problems with the delivery systems fitted in their aircraft.

With a perfectly straight face the USAF spokesman said, "Cluster bombing from our B-52s is very, very accurate. We are confident that 100% of our bombs are hitting the ground."

*

General Peter Cosgrove is a bloke who appears to have made a good fist of some tough jobs over the years. And the old bastard has a dry wit that gets displayed quietly.

He was being interviewed on radio about the forthcoming visit of a troop of Boy Scouts to a military base he was commanding at the time.

The woman interviewer asked what things the boys would be being taught during their visit to the base.

The general replied, "We're going to teach them climbing, canoeing, archery and shooting."

"Shooting! That's a bit irresponsible, isn't it?" she responded in a shocked voice.

"I don't see why," said Cosgrove. "They'll be properly supervised on the rifle range."

The woman pressed the point. "Don't you admit that this is a terribly dangerous activity to be teaching children?"

General Cosgrove remained quite placid. "I don't see how. We will be teaching them proper rifle discipline before they even touch a firearm."

By now the woman conducting the interview was becoming agitated. "But you're equipping them to become violent killers!" she exclaimed.

With perfect calm the general replied "Well, ma'am – you're equipped to be a prostitute, but you're not one, are you?"

The radio went silent and the interview ended.

*

I had a bit of a run-in with a tour guide at Pearl Harbour in Hawaii. He was a retired Navy serviceman. He told us he'd served in the Korean Police Action, still apparently holding to the line of the time that it wasn't officially a war.

He wasn't good with earlier conflicts either. Pointing across the harbour to the monument that marks the lost USS Arizona he said, "Here is where World War Two began on December 7, 1941."

"Excuse me," I interrupted. "That's just not right. Germany declared war on Poland in September 1939. That's usually regarded as the start of the War."

The guide changed colour a bit. Trying to salvage the situation he replied, "Okay – December '41 was the start of the War in the Pacific."

Before he could continue I interrupted again. "I don't think the Chinese would agree. Japan invaded there even before the German troops went into Poland."

"Really? I didn't know that!" was the response of several of the other people in the tour group.

The guide had lost them, and I hope that in some small way I was able to contribute to their understanding that the USA is not, in fact, the centre of the universe.

*

Todd is a US Marine I shared a few beers with while he was on leave from service in Iraq. He's a down-to-earth old bastard who proves not all Yanks are as bad as their stereotype.

By his own admission, a lot of his colleagues in uniform have only the sketchiest of ideas as to why they're actually in the Middle East.

"Because we were told to be," is what Todd reckons most of his buddies would reply if asked.

His own analysis is rather more interesting. Whether you agree with him or not, he expresses it succinctly.

"Got to admit," Todd said to me, "We stuffed the place up back in 2003. Our government is run by a bunch of businessmen. We're back in Iraq now on the 'you broke it, you bought it' principle."

*

Lawyers seem to be about the most unpopular of all of the so-called 'professionals'. I know of one who moved to a career in politics (thereby not noticeably improving the esteem of his occupation). When he scored a position as a Cabinet Minister for the first time he introduced himself to his new staff by admitting he's "part of the 98% of lawyers that give the rest a bad name".

For whatever reason, the whole worldwide explosion in litigation looks very much like it started in the USA.

Let's face it – this is the country where a woman sued a fast food restaurant because she slipped in a puddle of soft drink that she'd *just spilled herself*. And where another woman sued a department store after she tripped over her own child in one of their aisles.

There was the campervan driver who put the vehicle into 'cruise control' then climbed back out into the living area to pour a drink. After it ran off the road and into a tree he sued the campervan company for not explaining adequately that he was still supposed to steer the thing.

Worst of all I think was the idiot who tried to pick his nose with a power drill while it was operating. He tore a massive rip into the side of his face (I've seen the photos and they're not pretty), and then tried to sue the drill manufacturer because the tool didn't carry a warning sticker.

Silly manufacturer – imagine not printing in large friendly letters "Do Not Insert In Nostril While Drill Bit Is In Motion".

Here's a scary statistic I found in an old law textbook (I was really bored and desperate for something to read at a friend's place, okay?). In 1987 – that's over twenty years ago – there were on average over 12 million lawsuits filed in the US every year.

That's one legal action for every dozen people – men, women and children, in the entire country. I really hate to think what the figure is now.

*

I love the story of the Scottish country copper who pulled over a slick London lawyer who'd ignored a Stop sign.

The lawyer waved a dismissive hand at the constable. "There was no traffic about. I slowed down and looked around. It was perfectly safe. Can you tell me what difference it makes that I didn't actually stop?"

"Step oot o' the car, please sir," directed the policeman. The lawyer reluctantly complied. "Noo face the car and stand wi' yer legs apart and yuir hands on the roof o' the vehicle."

"See here! What's this about?" protested the driver.

"Please do as yuir directed, sir." Again the lawyer grudgingly complied. The copper started to tap his truncheon on the roof of the car. "Noo, sir, there's no traffic about. It'd be perfectly safe fer me tae start gie'in ye a guid whackin' wi' this peace-keepin' device. Havin' inflicted a couple o' blows to yuir person, I could slow down an' look around before continuin', or I could stop. Do ye reckon ye'd be aware o' the difference?"

*

I've read and heard a lot of debate at different times and in different places about 'fixed' speed cameras.

I don't mean 'fixed' in the racing sense i.e. deliberately interfered with to produce an artificial result, although that's not an unknown allegation either. I mean the unmanned cameras that are fixed permanently in one position and automatically photograph any vehicle exceeding the speed limit.

The theory is that they act as a deterrent. Of course, deterrents only work if you know they're there and the cameras, while not camouflaged, are not exactly stand-out obvious either. What's more, familiarity breeds contempt and most people who drive past a camera on a regular basis will soon forget that it's there.

I suppose if you keep getting booked for speeding in the same place time and time again you'll eventually lose your licence. That's a bit of a deterrent for some drivers. But if someone is so dumb, or so casual about speed limits that they repeatedly get busted in the same spot without learning from it, they're just as likely to not worry about driving without a licence.

The alternative and widely held view is that speed cameras are revenue raisers, not life savers. Speeding fines generate plenty of dollars for government.

The actual location of these 'fixed' cameras is worth considering. They're usually in heavy traffic but relatively low risk areas. You're less likely to find them in regular accident 'black spots'.

It's hard not to be a cynical old bastard. Especially when you've heard the explanation that a senior police officer (in a city which better remain anonymous) gave to a young constable: "You can't get money off a dead motorist."

*

Huw works for the British police, taking the calls that come in on their 999 emergency number (their equivalent of Australia's 000 and the USA's 911).

He told me about a call he took one night from a guard on a train heading south from Weston-Super-Mare. The guard had been threatened by two blokes armed with knives, who demanded that the train be stopped as they wanted to go north, not south.

When the guard explained that the train couldn't actually go in reverse to where they wanted, they pulled the Emergency Stop cord, forced open a door and jumped out, at which point the guard had called 999 to report the incident.

Huw asked if there were any witnesses, and over the phone heard the announcement over the train's PA system asking if anyone had seen the attempted hijacking and was prepared to talk to the police.

Soon after, someone came onto the phone to talk to him – a very drunk eighteen year old girl who was celebrating her birthday. She demanded that Huw wish her many happy returns before she'd tell him anything. He patiently complied, and after she flirted with him for a while longer he managed to get a useful story from her.

The two guys with the knives were brothers, they'd been involved in a scuffle near the Weston-Super-Mare station, and police there had put them on the train. It was only after the train got moving that they twigged it was going in the wrong direction.

In order to work out where the train had been stopped and the blokes had done their runner, Huw asked the guard if he recognized the location. When the answer was "No" he then asked the guard to describe what he could see.

There was a pause while the guard looked out of the train, then he came back onto the line.

"I can see the moon…"

*

I've seen this story in a couple of e-mails, but a Mississippi copper I met assures me it's true.

An old bastard who we'll call George was going to bed when his wife told him that he'd left the light on in the garden shed, which she could see from the bedroom window.

George went to turn the light off, but before he got there he noticed that there were people moving around in there, presumably nicking stuff.

He rang the police, who asked, "Are there any intruders in the house itself?"

When George replied that there weren't, the dispatcher advised that all patrols were busy, and George should just lock his door. An officer would be along "when one was available".

George said, "Okay", hung up, waited a minute or two, and then rang back.

"Hello. I called earlier to say there were people in my shed. Well, you don't have to worry about them now, cos I've just shot them." Then he hung up.

Within minutes there were three police cars, an armed response unit and an ambulance at George's place. The burglars were still in the shed and were caught red-handed.

The senior police officer berated George, "I thought you said you'd shot them!"

George shrugged. "I thought you said there was nobody available."

*

A good doctor is worth his or her weight in gold. Especially if they don't charge like that's what they're trying to make in a year. I've been told, and I willingly believe, that the biggest contributor to forcing up doctors' fees in the past few years has been the cost of insurance premiums.

That's fair enough, but some specialists in particular are charging so far over the odds that I reckon we're paying their personal liability insurance, home and contents insurance on a couple of oceanfront mansions, and car insurance on a fleet of BMWs driven by teenagers.

The best doctors are the ones who not only know their stuff, but also know how to talk to a patient. They're happy to tell you what's wrong, and what they can and can't do about it.

There are a lot who don't do that. I heard a very senior doctor being interviewed a while back, emphatically proclaiming that "patients should absolutely not be allowed to read their own files. That's private and personal information."

Yes it is, and if it's private and personal information about me I should bloody well be able to know what it contains. I did provide the raw data for it, after all!

A receptionist in a big hospital took a phone call one afternoon.

"I'm calling about a patient – Mrs. Lawson in Ward 3B. Can you tell me how she's doing please?" came the voice.

"I'm sorry, I can't really help you. I'll transfer you to the nurses' station in 3B," was the reply.

Put through to the appropriate extension, the question was repeated.

"Hang on," said the nurse, "I'll just check Mrs. Lawson's charts for you." She came back on the line fairly quickly and said "Mrs. Lawson is coming along nicely. Doctor is expecting to remove her stitches tomorrow and if she's able to eat properly and get up and move about safely she should be home within a week."

"Oh, that *is* good news, thank you," said the caller.

"Are you a relative?" asked the nurse.

"No, I'm Mrs. Lawson. I haven't been able to get that bastard doctor to tell me anything!"

*

I appreciate a doctor who can add a bit of wit to your conversations. John's a good one for that.

Several years back I had a very thorough series of tests done – the full medical suite. John called me in to "discuss the results".

As I sat in his office he nodded to himself as he looked through the numbers on my blood tests. "Well," he finally said, "I think you're actually in pretty fair shape for a man in his early sixties."

"Hang on, doc!" I protested. "I'm only 39!"

He looked me in the eye. "And what do you think I'm trying to tell you?" he asked.

I'm better now. Thanks, John.

*

A friend of mine who works as a nurse in a psych hospital told me about a particularly unfortunate patient there.

The girl had apparently done some seriously bad drug damage to herself in previous years, and now had lengthy spells during which she was convinced she was an orange.

She would roll around the floor of her room, and if anyone came in she'd scream and cry in panic that they'd come to peel her or squeeze the juice out of her.

When these spells passed she'd explain in a puzzled voice to anyone who'd listen that she'd "just had the trippiest dream…"

At one point she actually did need squeezing. Maybe it had something to do with all the rolling around the floor, but she developed a nasty abscess sore on her back which had to be drained.

As the hospital staff tried to treat her she started to thrash about and scream. It was both pain and panic I suspect.

Cunning old bastard of a doctor leaned to her ear and quietly said, "You can't feel anything – you're an orange, remember?"

It worked. She immediately went quiet and the nurses were able to clean her up nicely.

*

I heard this from a bloke who'd spent some time working for a real miserable old bastard of a farmer in the far north of Scotland.

The old sod didn't like getting wet – wouldn't even go outside in a mist. I know what the climate's like up there so I reckon he must have spent most of his life by the fireplace. But he wouldn't hear of his labourers having the chance to come in out of bad weather.

One especially foul day he said "Right, all of them as has oilskins (raincoats to you southern hemisphere city folk) can go out and pull turnips."
"And what about those of us that don't have oilskins?" asked one of the lads.
"Aye," said the old farmer, "You can do likewise."

*

Andy worked on a cattle property that regularly had visitors in on "Farm Stay Experience" holidays. It was quite a good lurk for the farmer – his guests cost less to fed than they paid for their vacation, and as part of their 'experience' they'd provide cost free, if usually unskilled labour.

Nothing too strenuous or remotely dangerous, but a good way to get done some of the little time-hungry jobs that proliferate on a working property.

While keeping an eye on the unpaid workforce for the boss, Andy loved to play up the 'wise old bushie' character. One of his favourites was to maneuver one of the visitors into asking him the time.

He'd take off his battered old Akubra, hold it up to the sun, sight along the brim to gauge how far above the horizon it was, and make his pronouncement: "Just short of quarter past two" for example.

Someone in the group would check their watch, and with awe in their voice advise, "It's a bit after ten past two! How do you *do* that?"

Andy would shrug as he put his Akubra back on. "Old bushman's trick," was all he'd say, keeping up the mystique.

One day the boss took him aside and said, "Andy, I've seen you do that a hundred times. I've seen you do it on sunny days, cloudy days, summer and winter, and I'm blowed if I know how you do it. What *is* the old bushman's trick?"

"Can you keep a secret, boss?" asked Andy. When he got a nod in reply, he took his Akubra off and held it up towards the sun.

Then he turned it around so the boss could see inside the crown. Stuck in the band on the inside of the brim was an old wristwatch, keeping perfect time.

"Easy when you know how," said the cunning old bastard.

*

Jan and Brian breed racehorses, and they've had a couple of good ones.

Prophet's Kiss was a fine stayer who picked up a few good Group One wins. She finished her racing career in the Melbourne Cup a few years ago.

Running her usual steady pace she was moving up through the field as other horses tired and slowed. About four hundred metres from the winning post the jockey heard a loud crack. Fearing the worst he tried to rein her in but she wouldn't be in that.

She kept up her pace to the end, overtaking a few more horses to finish eighth. Eighth in the Melbourne Cup is actually a paying finish for the owners. It was as though the stubborn old bastard of a horse had realized it was going to be her last race so she was determined to finance her future.

It worked out well. The winnings helped Jan and Brian improve their place, and Prophet's Kiss stayed with them, producing new generations of promising runners.

*

When Bill and Jenny first moved onto their property it was in need of quite a bit of work. At various times friends would come around to help.

In a paddock beside the house there were a couple of good-sized concrete water tanks, most of which had been sunk into the ground to help keep the water temperature down.

The metre or so of concrete tank walls that protruded were, like the tops of the tanks, pretty grubby and rough looking.

"A coat of paint might improve them," Jenny casually remarked in passing one day.

Bill filed that thought away, and when Jenny was off visiting her Mum for a few days he rounded up some mates and got busy.

He played it very cool when she got back and waited for her to notice his burst of creative genius. It didn't take long.

Well, it was hard to miss a paint job that created the illusion that someone had snuck into the paddock and buried two giant beer cans.

*

Eivol is an old Albanian who emigrated to Australia a few decades back. He did pretty well for himself, scratching together enough to buy his own tobacco farm.

He'd assembled a good irrigation system for his crop, but the nature of the local weather dictated that the ideal time for watering was the middle of the night.

So part of Eivol's routine was to climb on board his tractor at one o'clock in the morning, switch on the spotlight mounted on a pole attached to the cowling and trundle about checking the watering system.

"Wouldn't you know?" he said. "Dere is always a sprinkler in middle that not working!"

Of course, he couldn't turn off the system to unclog or replace the problem sprinkler head, because without the water running it would be impossible to identify which one was the offender.

So at one in the morning he'd be plodding about his tobacco plants, soaked to the skin.

"Typical!" he said to me, shaking his head. "All day I complain how this country too bloody hot. At night I go get wet and freeze!"

.o0o.

THE OLD BASTARD AT PLAY

Sport is a rich field in which to find the Old Bastard (pardon the pun). Playing or watching, sport is fundamentally about enjoyment and having a good time, or at least it's supposed to be. I know there are some miserable old bastards who take it all too seriously and get obsessed with winning at all costs.

The late legendary Liverpool manager Bill Shankly famously said "Football isn't a matter of life and death – it's much more important than that", but Shanks said a lot of funny stuff. I reckon he was the type of old bastard who'd say a lot of things with his tongue planted firmly in his cheek just to get a bit more newspaper column space for his team.

When that whole 'winning isn't everything, it's the only thing' attitude takes hold of someone for real, then I reckon what they're doing isn't sport any more. The fun's gone out of it, and they're engaging in a kind of small-scale warfare. I always get a kick out of someone like that being deflated by a funny old bastard with a healthier perspective.

*

I used to know a bloke named Al who was a 9 to 5 office worker, but would moonlight as a professional wrestler with one of the local Federations around Melbourne. Al was a big distinctive-looking blonde muscle man who could have easily used a successful wrestling gimmick as a mad Viking.

Unfortunately Al's main employer had made it clear that 'second jobs' were frowned upon, so he resorted to the time-honoured pro grappling tradition of wrestling under a black mask and using a stage name. It was something like "The Black Ninja" as I recall, and he wore one of those sinister masks that cover the whole head, like a balaclava with leather trim.

If you met Al the office worker, you'd find him a regular nice guy. Fond of a beer and a laugh, very much one of the boys. When he was working or training at his Other job, though, he was a whole different character. He became a real no-nonsense Hard Man.

Now, there's nothing wrong with taking your profession of wrestling seriously no matter the smirks a few of you are probably wearing right now. Fact is, it's hard yakka, especially if it's done well, and there's a lot of potential for serious injury if moves aren't executed properly.

So believe it or not a wrestling ring is no place for mucking around. But Al's problem was that he was taking himself too seriously outside of the ring. In training, and more particularly in the change room before and after matches, it was like he was starting to live the part of his tough guy character a little too well. I used to hang around with Al and a few of his ring cronies quite a bit, and they observed to me that he was getting worse as he got older.

One of these cronies, who for his own sake had better remain nameless, came up with a cracker of a practical joke to take some wind out of Al's sails. Just before a match one Friday night, while Al was paying a last-minute visit to the Gents the nameless old bastard grabbed the mask from out of The Black Ninja's gym bag. He quickly and liberally scribbled inside it with a dark green felt pen – one of those big buggers used for packing cases and the like, and then carefully put the mask back exactly where he found it.

Coming back a litre lighter, Al grabbed his mask and pulled it on. Now, even if he had thought to look inside he probably wouldn't have seen the dark pen marks on the black fabric, but being in a hurry to get to the ring he didn't spare a glance.

Al and his opponent put on a pretty decent 10 or 12 minute match under the hot lights, and they'd both been sweating heavily by the time the Black Ninja's hand was raised in victory and they headed back to the locker room.

There Al pulled his mask off and then realized all the boys were suddenly laughing at him. He got pretty fired up and was starting to look for someone to have Serious Words with, when he spotted himself in a mirror.

The perspiration from his scalp had caused the ink to run, and his blonde locks were now a definite green. The boys' laughter subsided as everyone waited for the explosion. Suddenly Al burst out laughing himself. "Bugger me," he said, "I look like the Joker!"

Luckily the pen wasn't a permanent marker and the green washed out over the weekend. Al mightn't have taken the gag so well if he'd had to turn up at the office on Monday explaining why he looked like a 'Batman' villain.

*

When you're playing a sport at anything less than the elite level you can find yourself trying to compete in a wide range of conditions. Small country towns and old established suburbs sometimes present unexpected challenges to the visitor.

I know of a golf course in one Victorian town that adjoins a rifle range. One particular fairway is right in the line of fire of anyone who happens to miss their target.

There's a polite agreement been reached between the two clubs. Golfers playing that hole must, before they walk the fairway, press a button near the tee that activates a warning bell in the shooting club.

There is a local rule at the golf club that that if your ball is shot out of the air you're allowed to replay the stroke without penalty. As far as I know, nobody's ever copped a stray bullet, so I can't say if a similar rule applies were someone to be pinged themselves while playing a stroke.

Cricket is also noted for variation in quality between grounds. I've heard several stories in Australia and overseas of cricket grounds where a large tree is on or inside the boundary. Others are located on sites that offer a playing surface that, in whole or in part, slope dramatically.

I've seen a concrete pitch with a crack in it so wide that you could stick a crammed pencil case in it, never mind Tony Grieg's borrowed fountain pen. There are rough country grounds where the pitch is a length of weather-worn carpet, or even weed matting.

But an old bastard who loves their sport puts up with that – it's all part of the game. And sometimes you get to play in places where the view or surroundings are grand enough to make up for the challenges.

I've played bowls at the foot of Ben Nevis in Scotland, and on greens with great panoramic views of the Derwent in Tasmania. All around Australia there are bowling greens, cricket pitches and footy fields with million dollar views of the beach and rolling surf.

Sometimes the view can be too distracting. Pete told me of a ground he'd played on which sat on a bit of a plateau overlooking a racecourse. The problem was that the wicket keeper in Pete's team was a mad keen punter.

Apparently he didn't stop many deliveries that day, and a fair number of those that he *did* stop were accidental – the ball clattering into him while he was looking downhill.

*

I reckon that in some ways our appreciation of sport has actually been spoiled by how good radio and television coverage has become. I've met a few people who've said they don't go to see matches or games (in a few different sports) because either they don't get as good a view, or they reckon it's too hard to follow the play without commentary.

That's what I'm getting at. We're so used to having every action described and every move analyzed that it's no longer necessary to really watch what's going on for ourselves. Take away that commentary and a lot of 'sports fans' couldn't tell you what they're watching or even, in the case of team sports, who.

So the commentators themselves have become an important part of the game – whatever your game is. A few of them have taken that, and themselves, too seriously. One of my pet peeves is the 'colour' or 'expert' commentator who's so enthused with his own wisdom and the sound of his own voice that he talks over the action instead of between it.

You know the situation I mean. The retired player or coach is explaining at length how things were done in their day, or should be done now. And when I say at length, I mean at length. The poor old 'play-by-play' commentator finally gets back on air and has to start with "And in the meantime, Smith has scored…"

Of course, over the years a lot of commentators have been funny old bastards. Some have been deliberate comedians, others funny without meaning to be.

A rugby league caller on Grafton radio quite a few years back came up with this gem during a local game. A close match right from the start, it got even more tense a few minutes from full-time when the home side scored a late penalty goal to level the scores. The enthusiastic caller shouted down the airwaves: "And now both sides have hit the front!"

In the same vein, I remember a Brisbane rugby league radio man a while ago (long enough that you could actually hear local games broadcast!) breathlessly informing his listeners that "with the score at Brothers 11, Valleys 11, one more point each and they'll be level!"

The same guy left a lot of us bemused the day he signed off with "That's the full time score here at Lang Park". There was a long silence, during which I suspect someone was making a frantic phone call from the studio. And then: "Sorry, that's the *half* time score here at Lang Park…"

*

Cricket seems to attract the commentators who might otherwise have looked for a career in stand-up comedy. In Australia Kerry "Skull" O'Keefe is perhaps most famous for his manic laugh, usually at his own jokes. I reckon he's also got a fine turn of phrase to complement a greater insight into the game than he's given credit for. Skull has released books and CDs taken from the funnier moments of his match commentary, but one I really enjoyed came when he was reflecting on playing alongside Doug Walters.

With great respect he described Walters as 'totally fair – he never sledged anyone', and described how Doug's unflappable presence, cigarette and stubby in hand, was a wonderfully calming influence in the dressing room between 10 a.m. and 6 p.m., defusing other players' stress with a laconic word or two.

What amazed and disconcerted Skull was that Doug could retain both this calm and his exceptional ability as a batsman despite his lifestyle outside match hours. It was dangerous to socialize with him, apparently.

"Even on game nights you'd be out till 4 a.m. drinking. And even if you didn't touch a cigarette yourself you did so much passive smoking you might as well have had a pack of your own. And he'd front up ten o'clock next morning right as rain while the rest of us were like dead men."

Skull described hanging around with Doug as "metabolically challenging".

In earlier days the likes of Max Walker and Ian Chappell have released books of stories and anecdotes good for a laugh, although they usually played their commentary straight. Their frequent microphone colleague Tony Greig was not, I think, trying to be deliberately funny the time he described a batsman "dancing down the mitch and pissing it."

There is a great tradition of humour among the English cricket commentators. The great Brian Johnston produced several books of anecdotes, recounting stories and funny moments from covering matches all over the world for many years. If you're a cricket fan I suggest you keep an eye out any time you're in a secondhand book store for any of Brian's work.

My own favourite though was John Arlott. A very astute reader of the game, who spoke with a classical refined BBC accent, Arlott also had a wry dry wit. But he had such an air of class and dignity that it wasn't always immediately obvious when he was being witty.

I reckon he's the only bloke who could have escaped discipline from the BBC after describing a mediocre day's play by a New Zealand bowler as follows: "Bob Cunis – his bowling today has been much like his name – not quite one thing nor the other."

*

It's become commonplace for sports people to turn to careers in the media once they've hung up their boots/bat/trunks/equipment of choice. Not just as game commentators, but as newsreaders, journalists and public speakers.

Some are naturals and prove themselves comfortable and capable behind a microphone or in front of a camera right away. Others take a while, but persist and gradually grow into their new role.

But there are some who just don't seem to belong in the position, and seem unwilling or unable to learn.

Ilie Nastase has had a fair bit of experience as a tennis commentator since he retired his racquet. Apparently he's not too bad at calling live action. But the demands of a more formal career in the media seem to be beyond him. He struggles with difficult tasks like reading from a script.

The Nasty One's best effort came at the Laureus World Sports Awards. These awards are held in particularly high regard in Europe, and the presentation night is right up there with the Oscars in terms of prestige.

Proudly clutching the award he was supposed to present, Ilie faced the ceremony guests and large television audience.

Reading directly from the teleprompter screen he enthusiastically announced, "The winner of the Sportsperson With A Disability Award is… Open The Envelope!!"

It may have been the reaction of the audience, or the non-arrival on stage of Mr. or Ms Envelope that prompted him to actually think about what he was supposed to be doing.

If the judges at Laureus ever decide stupidity should be counted as a disability Ilie just might win the award himself.

*

If commentators are great sources of fun in sport, so too are fans. Barracking for your team, rubbishing the opposition, passing comments on the ref or umpire – they're all opportunities for witty old bastards to shine.

Back in the days of World Series Cricket I was sitting on the Hill at the Gabba, along with a huge crowd of other sunburned drunks, watching Australia get decimated by a Rest Of The World side. Chief destroyer on the day was South African Garth Le Roux who took a swag of wickets for not many runs.

After yet another of his wickets someone on the Hill shouted, "Go back to France, ya bastard!"

From elsewhere came the response, "He's not French – he's African."

The first voice replied angrily, "Of course he's bloody French – what else could he be with a name like Le Roux?"

From somewhere down the front came another voice: "He might be Australian…"

The whole Hill went quiet while we pondered that one, before the same voice continued, "He might be a Kang Le Roux".

*

Several years later, the scene is on the other side of the country. The West Indies are touring, and have been dominating the Aussies. After taking a good bag of wickets in the first Test, Merv Hughes' season had fallen away badly. By the time of the Perth Test he was really struggling.

Trudging back to field near the boundary after another unsuccessful over, big Merv wasn't best pleased when some wag in the crowd shouted the question "Hey Merv – how many wickets ya taken since Brisbane?"

Not even bothering to turn around, Hughes has waved a two-fingered salute in the direction of the voice, which promptly replied "Ha! Ya can't even count – it's only *one*!"

*

In the hospitality tent at Adelaide Oval, I was having a quiet drink with a former Test player.

"Do you want a glass with that stubby?" asked the girl serving the Coopers.

He looked at her as if she was dopey.

"It's *in* glass," he pointed out before downing a hearty swig.

*

I was at a country racetrack in South Australia. It was getting late in the day, and many of the punters had taken a few too many drinks on board.

The favourite in race six was well beaten, having been boxed into a pack of horses for most of the journey.

After the finish the unhappy jockey was obliged to take his horse past a particularly disgruntled group of race-goers who'd obviously lost money on the result.

One of them obviously figured he could have done a better job of the ride. He called out to the hoop "Hey, ya mug! Didn't you see that gap that opened up in front of you 400 metres from the finish?"

The jockey barely looked up as he replied, "Yeah I saw it. I guess you didn't notice – the gap was going faster than we were."

*

Wimbledon is regarded as a very Proper place. The Open there is regarded as the most distinguished of tennis tournaments to win.

Other than their ongoing frustration at the lack of a genuine local contender to win the event (Andy Murray being a Scot, *not* an Englishman, thank you!), the English crowd is usually quite restrained and respectful. Enthusiastic, yes, but polite.

It's hard to picture someone being noisy and boisterous, far less aggressive, when their match-time snack is strawberries and cream.

Even the travelling fans seem mostly to embrace the idea of low key support. That said, one of the cleverest placards I've ever seen was being waved aloft at Wimbledon several years ago.

Aussie hero Pat Cash was in a match with long-time rival Ivan Lendl. It was at a time when they were both playing excellent tennis and the match was expected to be a cracker. Both players had a strong following.

Australian fans have a bit of a reputation for rowdiness, even at the tennis, but at Wimbledon the behaviour is usually very good. Abuse is not tolerated by the local officials, and even the positive support has to be kept pretty unobtrusive. One Aussie wit in the stands at courtside expressed his feelings about the match though by holding up a large sign which read "I'll take Cash over a Czech any day!"

*

My old mate Scotty has a neat turn of phrase. Before the first bounce of an AFL game we were watching I asked him if he was confident of his team's chances.

"Mate, they're a concrete slab," he told me. "You could put your house on them!"

Almost inevitably they lost. Admittedly it was only by two points, but they lost.

"What happened to the concrete slab?" I asked Scotty.

"Nothing wrong with the slab," he replied. "Just dodgy foundations."

*

You meet a lot of funny old bastards playing lawn bowls. Some of them are a lot younger than the stereotype might have you expect a lawn bowler to be. Often times these younger ones turn out to be guns – the average age of the Australian national team is a lot lower now than it was a few years back.

Happily though, not all of them take the game or themselves too seriously, even if they're very good at it. It was an excellent bowler in his early 20's who said to me "I figure I'm the second best bowler in this club. Everyone else reckons they're the best."

The funniest bowlers I've found are the ones who direct their wit at themselves, particularly if they're having an off day.

A few years back at Canberra Bowling Club I was up against a bloke who was having a really dirty day. None of his shots were coming near the mark, especially the big drives and on-shots he was trying to use to get out of trouble. He was getting crankier and crankier, muttering to himself. I thought 'I better watch this joker – he's starting to change colour'.

An end or two later he played a thundering drive, missed the mark by two feet and took out his own best bowl. He stood on the mat, hands on hips, and said, "Fair dinkum – if it wasn't for gravity I couldn't hit the ground!"

I couldn't help myself – I cracked up laughing, then so did he. Funny thing is he started playing better after that. A good laugh is good therapy.

In a similar vein, I was playing at Moorooka more recently against a bloke who, while bowling pretty well, just wasn't getting the 'rub of the green'.

My bowl would topple in to win a close measure, and two ends later his bowl would topple out to lose one. I'd get a lucky 'wick' (ricochet off another bowl) to pinch shot, and then he'd get a faint nick to turn his own good shot into a dud.

He was frustrated but taking it in good spirit. After watching a seemingly perfect delivery get held up by a sudden strong gust of wind and finish two feet short of its target he turned to me with a shrug and said, "Mate, if it was raining soup I'd be out here with a fork."

Another bloke I was sharing a green with had to endure a similar run of wretched luck.

"Fair dinkum," he growled through clenched teeth, "I reckon if I fell into a vat full of nipples I'd come out sucking me thumb!"

*

Up in the Adelaide hills I had a skipper named Dave who was a real character. He was a Pom with a great sense of humour, but he could drive his team-mates mad. Any team of Dave's could be guaranteed to finish a 21-end game long after every other rink, because he'd spend so long each end analyzing the lay of the bowls and giving detailed directions to his team-mates.

What he was directing was usually tactically very sound, but it was also frequently bleeding obvious, especially to quite experienced bowlers like most of his team-mates. Often too, he wouldn't just give directions, he'd give options, all in great detail.

I think that sometimes he got so caught up in analyzing a situation he lost track of time and the requirement to actually *play* a shot in reasonably short order. "It's not bloody chess!" he was heatedly told on more than one occasion.

I remember one game where Dave walked around the bowls several times, head down, calling various possible shots that might be tried. Finally, on the fourth or fifth "…or alternatively, you could try…" Andy, who was on the mat, just went ahead and played the shot he'd had in mind anyway. It wasn't one of the ones suggested thus far.

Dave had his back to the mat and was still talking when Andy's bowl rolled past his feet, took a little wick and came to rest in the perfect position. Without breaking his sentence Dave nodded and turned back to Andy saying, "…or *that* would work, too."

*

I was playing in a pennants game one afternoon. My foursome was doing alright, but I noticed that late in a lot of ends our skipper seemed to either speed us up or slow us down quite dramatically.

It was starting to rattle me so eventually I asked him what was going on. He looked a bit sheepish and said, "Sorry, I've only just given up smoking," and walked away.

I puzzled over this for a bit, then a couple of ends later I noticed that the skipper on the rink next to us was smoking a pipe, and it was a richly aromatic tobacco he was enjoying. Our skipper was working hard to ensure that our ends were co-ordinated as closely as possible to theirs so that he could spend as much time as he could standing downwind of the pipe, enjoying a 'passive'.

*

Big Bruce is an impatient old bastard, and that's not a good trait in a golfer. One particular day out on the greens Bruce and his group kept being held up on the back nine by the foursome ahead of them, who were careful, meticulous putters.

Bruce's playing partners weren't bothered. The leading group was never so slow as to require 'playing through', but Bruce kept getting tetchier and tetchier.

Over the last few holes he kept yelling at the preceding players to "Hurry up! Hurry up!"

He usually timed his shouts as they attempted to putt. Stupid really, as it put them off their stroke and actually slowed them down further.

Finally they were done, and Bruce and his by now mortified partners were able to play the last hole.

As they walked up the fairway, the clouds that had been quietly gathering all afternoon finally burst open. It was the sort of serious downpour that will leave bruises if you stay out in it for long. When they neared the green Big Bruce was able to catch one last sight of his golf ball as the waters carried it down a slope and into a fresh stream.

Nobody said much within Bruce's earshot, but later discussion amongst his playing partners held this incident as proof that if there isn't actually a God of Golf, there is at least some spirit of justice watching over the game.

*

I liked the definition of golf I heard in a bar a while back: an endless series of tragedies obscured by the occasional miracle, made tolerable by the drinks afterwards.

The same sad soul lamented that golf is the only sport where your most feared opponent is yourself.

"No matter how badly you're playing, it's always possible to get worse," he said.

*

An extremely enthusiastic reporter was interviewing Phil Mickelson after a tournament win.

"You're incredible, spectacular!" gushed the reporter. "Your name is synonymous with great golf. You really do know your way round a course! What's your secret?"

Mickelson looked slightly embarrassed and explained to the reporter, as if imparting one of the great secrets of life, "The holes are numbered."

*

Most team nicknames are at least positive, if not seriously grand. Every sport has them - you know the type: Lions, Hawks, Chargers, Storm, Patriots, Firebirds, Mighty Ducks even.

There are a few interesting exceptions around. Rugby league's South Sydney Rabbitohs take their moniker from the blokes who used to go round the streets and pubs selling the animals they'd shot in order to raise money for the Club in its early days. It's worth recalling that fact at times when the side is playing like a bunch of bunnies.

The most self-deprecating nickname I've ever heard belongs to the baseball team from Long Beach State University. Maybe they don't like the idea of having too much to live up to, as their side is officially called The Dirtbags.

*

For someone who's spent so much time in aeroplanes I'm still a lousy flier. Actually, I don't mind being up in a plane, but there are three bits that make me tense. Take-off and landing both see me white-knuckled and desperately trying to distract myself.

The other time I hate is when some insensitive bastard in the cockpit comes over the loudspeakers to say, "Hello everyone – we're now traveling at 39,000 feet…"

Don't tell me that! I really do <u>not</u> want to know how far away solid earth is.

Nor am I very comfortable on the odd occasions when I've heard an announcement like "We've been asked to maintain a holding pattern, so we'll be circling for a while to use up excess fuel."

As far as I'm concerned the only time a plane has too much fuel on board is when it's actually on fire.

I wasn't made to feel any easier when it was explained to me what pilots and air traffic controllers have in common. If a pilot stuffs up badly, the chances are that everyone on board the plane will die. If an air traffic controller stuffs up badly, the chances are that everyone on board the plane will die.

Apparently though, the basic fundamental rule of flying is the same whether you're piloting a fighter jet, an airliner, a glider or a helicopter.

Try to stay in the middle of the air. Don't go too near the edges of it.

The edges can be recognized by the appearance there of things like buildings, trees, mountains, ground, sea or interstellar space. Rookie pilots are warned that all of these things are much more difficult to fly in than air.

I suppose in one way mankind does have a perfect record with aviation. We've never yet left a plane up there.

*

I heard a great interview with a seventy-plus year old stunt pilot down in Tasmania.

Asked why he was still doing barrel rolls and loop-the-loops at his time of life, he replied, "I do it for me health."

The interviewer must have looked puzzled, as the old bloke went on to explain, "I suffer from hardening of the arteries. I have to fly upside down occasionally to keep the blood flowin' to me brain."

*

Bill admits to being a 'white knuckled flyer' like me, even after literally hundreds of hours in aeroplanes. He described his worst experience in the air.

"We were in a little thirteen seater, which ran into a storm. The turbulence was bad enough, but the biggest problem was that the pilot had left his cockpit door open.

So all of us back in the cabin could see the red alarm light flashing above his seat. What was worse, we could hear the mechanical voice from the console going 'Warning! Warning!'

One of the other passengers was a priest, and when we landed he reckoned it was the most enthusiastic and sincere prayer meeting he'd ever run!"

*

I used to play football ('soccer' some of you probably call it) alongside another old bastard who'd often come across as a real tough guy, even though he had the proverbial heart of gold. Hambone was a truckie by profession, and pretty much looked the stereotypical part: muscles and a beer gut, tattoos, pulling his jersey on over a blue singlet just before the game started. And he had a vocabulary that was ten shades of blue.

He'd play the game hard but fair, to the best of his ability. His problem was that he didn't have much of a turn of speed.

I remember one bizarre game we played against a team from the local Deaf Society. They were way too good for us anyway, but it didn't help that they'd be signaling to each other in sign language. That meant we had more trouble than usual working out where a ball was likely to go and who we should be marking.

Hambone was having a particularly bad time in defence. His opposing winger seemed not only one-and-a-half times Hambone's size, but at least one-and-a-half times his speed, too. He was a big natural athlete, and he was literally running rings around our poor old bastard.

Frustrated at having been left flat on the grass yet again, Hambone let fly at him with one of the foulest gobfuls I've ever heard anywhere, anytime. Having casually slotted another goal the big bloke trotted back to where Hambone was still mouthing off. When Ham stopped for breath the guy said calmly, "I'm not deaf you know. I just work with these blokes."

Looking up at him, Hambone went quite pale and managed a quiet, "Oops… er… sorry mate." The other guy grinned and stuck out a paw to help him back to his feet.

"No worries," he said. Still, I reckon he could afford to be generous. He and his mates put seven goals past us that day.

*

Like I said, Hambone really wasn't as tough as he seemed. One time during a game I landed real hard and dislocated my shoulder. Hurt like blazes but it had happened before and I knew what to do. Hambone was the nearest bloke to me, and he was staring wide-eyed at me. We wore striped jerseys, and the snug-fitting one I wore apparently had a definite zigzag effect happening at the top of the sleeve.

I held out my hand to him. "Grab my arm and pull," I said. Staring at my shoulder he gave a little whimper, "I can't do that – it'll hurt!"
"It hurts *now* ya dill!" I answered.

Hambone reluctantly grabbed my wrist and gave a timid little tug. By now I was really feeling it and didn't want to mess about any longer. "Not like that – put yer back into it!" I shouted. As he gave my arm a decent yank I pulled back hard the other way.

It worked a treat. Popped back in like I knew it would and I felt better right away. Not 100%, but a helluva lot better. The only problem was that my shoulder had snapped back into its socket with a loud resounding 'crack'. Hambone promptly went white and fainted.

We had to carry him off. I went over to thank him when he came to. He scowled at me. "You bastard," he said, "I thought I'd torn yer arm off!"

*

British football club managers have given us some of the greatest quotes in sport. I mentioned Liverpool's Bill Shankly earlier. Manchester United's Sir Alex Ferguson is another. He famously described Dennis Wise as "the sort of man who could start a fight in an empty room."

I've also long admired the wit of the Scot Tommy Docherty. While he was boss of Manchester United in the 1970's the team went through a bit of a rough patch, and some unflattering things were said about 'Doc' in a few newspapers.

There was some concern that he might respond by barring the media from the club. Asked about this prospect Tommy replied, "I've always said there's a place for the press."

Then after a pause he added, "It just hasn't been dug yet."

*

Over the past several years trivia competitions have become really popular. They're good fund-raisers for schools and charities, and get bums on seats regularly at a lot of clubs and pubs. They've caught on so well that there are quite a few people around who get paid by pubs, businesses or whatever to run them.

It's a living for some of them, and fair enough too for the good ones – they're entertainers in their own right. What's more, the best of them write their own questions and do their own research – more than just pulling dubious stuff off the internet.

It takes time, especially for those who run several shows per week. Knowing that some people will attend more than one of those shows means that the soft option of re-using questions isn't available, so the quizmaster may be preparing 150 brainteasers or more per week. So much for the comments from some players that, "Jeez, you've got an easy job, only working a couple of hours a week!"

The biggest advantage of putting in that time on research is that if anyone *does* challenge an answer, the host can come up with a better response than, "I don't know – it's just what it says here on my sheet."

I reckon the best I've seen is PK in Brisbane. He's a good host, tells a good story, and can have a laugh at his own expense without losing any credibility. He's also raised a lot of money for charity passing around the hat at his regular venues.

One of the things that make a good quiz is the standard of the questions. You've got to get a balance between too easy and too hard, so you can sort out a clear winner without leaving anyone feeling like a humiliated dill.

In a round of ten questions there ought to be, on average, about five questions that an ordinary team of folks who read a bit, watch a bit of TV, and remember a bit from school days might reasonably get. Add another two a bit tougher, two more that are tougher still – things that really test the memory, or reasoning, or how thoroughly they keep up with current affairs.

And at least one that's a real tester – something that requires real depth of knowledge. They're the questions that will provide the winner on the night. Ideally though, everyone will have had fun, and some will actually go away having learned one or two things that might stick in their head for future reference, even if only at another quiz night!

Really good trivia hosts get this sort of result. They get known, and they attract customers, which is good business for the people who hire them.

*

At the other end of the scale I've found the odd host who really seems to just be doing the job to show off their own cleverness. There was a guy at a tavern in Canberra some years ago who was like that. He was an Honours student in something at Australian National University, and he delighted in looking smarter than other people.

His questions were often really obscure, and he'd nit-pick on the accuracy of answers. After several drinks one night he admitted that his ambition was to come up with a quiz one night where nobody got *any* answers right.

Needless to say, numbers fell away steadily and the tavern eventually got rid of the smug bastard. The damage to their reputation was done, though, and the poor sod who replaced him struggled to get back the numbers of people who'd gotten fed up and gone elsewhere for a night's entertainment.

*

With the proliferation of these quiz nights it's not just presenters who find them lucrative. There are individuals and teams who 'do the circuit' in their home city.

Some follow a particular presenter from venue to venue. I don't think it's necessarily loyalty. At least some of them expect to hear the same questions repeated and so get an edge on their less traveled opponents.

Of course, as I said before, a good quizmaster doesn't fall into that trap, even if not recycling questions at different venues does mean lot more work!

Other players are more strictly mercenary, and work a regular routine of the quizzes that offer the best prizes. They also keep alert for news of events at well-off schools or sports clubs, political fundraisers etc. where there's a reasonable expectation of generous sponsors donating good prizes.

I know of one team of retirees in Brisbane who've developed a fearsome reputation. They have a 'win at all costs' attitude that grates on some of the teams around them who play for a fun night out. They're notoriously regular at the same three or four pubs and clubs every week. Someone in their team must also haunt Community Billboards and local newspapers, too. I've seen and heard of them at fundraisers in suburbs right across Brisbane.

They're a team strong on just about every subject category you could think of – I think there are retired teachers and lecturers among them. Equally clearly someone (or more) among them read the daily paper from cover to cover and has an excellent memory.

Their only evident weakness was modern pop music. That was remedied when their team expanded to include the grand-daughter of one of the original members. It was worth dividing the spoils by one extra share to further boost their likelihood of winning.

I've heard it suggested on some particularly frustrating evenings that their winnings should be reported to Centrelink in the hope of having their pensions reduced.

*

I've heard a lot of odd descriptions for wines over the years. Some of them have been surprisingly, or even disconcertingly, accurate

There was a Bordeaux red I was introduced to a while back that was described as having "barnyard aromas". To be precise, it smelled like something nasty you might step in while crossing a barnyard.

Fortunately the taste was nothing like what your nose had prepared you for. It was big and interesting, but not at all like something that a cow had already consumed and digested.

A lot of the 'professional' wine descriptions seem weird and unlikely until you encounter an example. The idea of wine tasting or smelling like "buttered toast" seems ridiculous until you try a good chardonnay that's been well aged in French oak barrels.

It's not just wine that invites interesting descriptions. There are for instance some curiously flavoured vodkas out there to challenge the palate.

One of the more potent of these is becherovka, which is infused with cinnamon and other spices. I'd call it strong, quite hot, and quite sweet.

Michael was rather more descriptive.

"My first impression was that I'd had my tongue squared off," he said. "Then there were ranks of cinnamon soldiers running down my tongue, scraping off layers as they went. Finally, as you swallow, a scimitar swings across the back of your throat taking out your tonsils."

You might not have picked it from his critique, but Michael has become a keen drinker of becherovka.

*

Many of you will know of 'Passion Pop'. It's been around for years. For those who've not encountered it, it's a fruity white wine with bubbles. These days it even comes with citrus flavouring. It has its fans, though I'm not one of them. Its distinguishing characteristics are that it's sweet, fizzy, and cheap.

So it was disconcerting to find it listed as a Chinatown restaurant's "Wine Of The Month".

Worse still, it was being promoted at the "special price" of $22.50 per bottle. (The last time I noticed it in a bottle shop it was about $6 – I guess a mark up of over 250% is pretty special.)

As a final eyebrow raiser, it was described as "sparking wine". I do hope that was just a typo and they'd misspelled 'sparkling'. Otherwise I guess someone misinterpreted the name 'Passion Pop' and the term 'sparking wine' is a polite Chinatown expression for the old Aussie slang 'leg-opener'.

*

Rugby union players are thought to be a bit brighter than players of other codes of football. By themselves and their fans, at least.

It has something to do with so many of them having private school and University backgrounds, I think. That hasn't helped all of them, though.

I heard this story from a recently retired international, and having met one of the blokes involved I see no reason to doubt it.

Two of his team-mates were sharing a flat in the UK while playing as 'guests' of a club there.

They were watching the television when a news story came on featuring an extended interview with then-Soviet leader Mikhail Gorbachev.
"What's that thing on his head? It looks like a big patch of ink," observed one.
"That's a birthmark," answered the other.
"Oh. Right, I see," was the reply, followed by, after a thoughtful pause, "I wonder how long he's had that."

*

There's a great Australian tradition of not just going to watch the cricket, but making a Big Day Out of it. These days with the price of admission, the inflated price of food and the cost of plastic cups of mid-strength beer, you might as well – it's making a Big hole in your wallet!

One of the more interesting expressions of this is the Themed Look. This is when a group of cricket lovers (well, people attending a game together) all wear matching, or at least very similar, outfits.

I've seen numbers of nuns, hordes of Hawaiians, and masses of Mexicans. Even a battalion of Benauds (in beige suits and Richie masks). One year there was an influx of Indians (of the cowboy movie variety, not the sub-continent citizens).

It was a hot day, and quite a few blokes had stripped down to feathered head-dress, fringed vest – a couple were real chamois leather but most were cheap imitations, and shorts or swimwear. Sitting in the sun, several were cultivating serious red skins to go with their outfits.

There was one bloke who really disturbed me, though. Obviously lacking pocket space, he'd wedged – and I use the word carefully – his mobile phone down the back of his very brief swimming trunks. (At least, I *hope* it was <u>his</u> phone!)

I don't want to try to imagine what it would have been like talking on that phone!

*

I was in the US just before their football season was due to start.

There was a sports program on the TV, in the bar where I was enjoying a quiet drink.

Two pundits were deep in earnest conversation about which of two options should start the season at quarterback for the Cleveland Browns. One option was a journeyman who'd been reliable but unspectacular at a few clubs, the other a rookie who had potential but some questions around 'big game temperament'.

A bloke at the bar looked up disdainfully and said, "If the Good Lord Himself came down and played quarterback for them I'd still have ten bucks on whoever they were playing."

Harsh, I thought. Witty, but harsh.

*

Fencing isn't the most high-profile sport in the world, but it's actually pretty cool to try.

The oddest place I've ever had lessons was on board a cruise ship, sailing up the Baltic Sea. We had a really good coach, and learning to thrust and parry while keeping your balance as the ship rolled underneath you was a challenge!

And yes, we were well equipped with lots of padding, and safety tips on the swords.

I've got a few friends who are really into the sport, and would occasionally practice in my back yard on weekends just for fun. It let them indulge their inner pirate, I suppose.

Because they weren't being serious or competitive, the practices featured a lot of noise, Errol Flynn impressions, and not a lot of proper padding. Safety tipped blades, but you'd have to look closely to know it.

My neighbours Conrad and Helene were used to it. They were used to all sorts of things living next to me, I suppose. But Conrad delighted in telling me about some visitors they'd had who'd noticed the goings-on over the fence.

The husband had gone out onto Conrad's balcony for a smoke, then called back inside, "Strewth! The neighbours are fighting – and they're usin' swords!"

"Get back inside then, you fool!" his wife ordered. "You don't want to be called up as a witness!"

Conrad and Helene looked at each other and bit their tongues.

*

I was watching a very big boxing match on the TV in a very crowded pub.

It was very much promoted as a 'good guy' versus 'bad guy' contest. That's unusual for boxing these days – much more associated with professional wrestling, and since the 1930's boxing has tried to cultivate an image of being a Serious Sport, while the other squared circle events are 'Sports Entertainment'.

This bout was a notable exception though, and the guys involved played up to their public perceptions very well.

As the fight wore on, it was interesting to watch and listen to the people in the crowd talking about who'd won each round and why.

Much of that was coloured by the whole hero/villain emotional filter, especially among those I'll call the casual, 'Big Event' watchers. But there were a number of serious boxing fans there too, including some ex-fighters, who were trying to 'call' the fight as honestly as they could.

As I watched and listened (and considered my own assessment of what I was seeing round by round) I was struck by how widely opinions were differing on what was happening on screen.

We were all watching the same event at the same time, but seeing it in totally different ways. No wonder sporting events that are decided not by points scored (like bull's-eyes or racquet sports) but rather by the verdict of judges are the ones most dogged by controversy.

Try to think of that next time you're irate at a result you disagree with in the boxing, or gymnastics, or the figure skating. Judging is easy – everyone does it. Getting it 'right', that's different. You really can't please all of the people all of the time.

*

I know that there's corruption in sport. The bigger the competition the bigger the temptation, I suppose. The mess swirling around the top of soccer's governing body FIFA seems to be pretty good evidence of that.

But sadly, it goes down to the much lower levels of the game too.

Football isn't huge in India, as far as I can make out. But for those who play it, like Bill Shankly said, it's more than a matter of life and death. More than a matter of honesty, at least.

The last round of games in the Goan Second Division in 1994 saw two teams level on points. Both sides were playing opponents they were expected to beat, so the title was going to come down to goal averages. Both of them went looking for big scores.

Both got them, too, with big efforts in their respective second halves.

How big? Well, the Wilfred Leisure side won by a handy 55-1. (This is soccer, remember.)

Not enough though, as Curtorim Gym's opponents also managed to collapse dramatically. 61-1 dramatically.

The Goan Football Association decided that it was "cheating on a monstrous level" and suspended all four teams for a year.

I reckon that's actually pretty lenient!

*

Meredith and I idly wandered into the Annual Northern California BMX Championships. Well, it was a quiet afternoon for us, nothing obviously better to do, and we happened to be literally walking right by where they were being held.

I've never paid a lot of attention to BMX. I figured it was a kid's sport, and if it kept them off the street and out from under passing cars (especially mine) then that was a Good Thing.

I guess the sport's been around for a while, and some people have grown up with it, because the Championships competitors included no shortage of big burly blokes pushing bikes, clearly their own, that looked like they barely came up to their thighs.. There were probably some adult women riders too, we just weren't there at the right time to see them. The oldest age range we saw racing was the 35-40 year old category but there were definitely guys older than that strolling around in their fluorescent racing suits.

Some of the outfits were works of art. A lot were walking billboards for as many sponsors as could be squeezed onto the human body. There was one bloke who I was honestly sure was dressed as a clown. 'Rodeo has them, why not BMX?' I figured.

Several guys looked more like they belonged on growling 600CC+ motorcycles than pedal-pushers. A couple of them did roll past us on big Harley Davidsons, trophy clutched under the arm and dinky BMX bike somehow tied precariously on the back.

There's a lot of money, passion, and commitment tied up in it, judging by some of the kit we saw in some of the competitors' family marquees. The various mobile homes, trailers and other big vehicles that had transported those families to Roseville, California added to that body of evidence.

There were, of course, plenty of kids there too, zipping about hither and yon, and not just on the competition track. The most junior competition we actually saw was the seven-year-old novices, but judging by the size of some of the sponsors' logo-bedecked munchkins we saw, I wouldn't be surprised to learn that there were younger categories.

As we made our way out through the car park there was a family coming back in from the nearby convenience store. Young son, still in his racing suit, I'm sure no more than seven, asked if he could go play with his mates now please?

His mother nearly bit his head off. Thankfully she stopped just short of laying a hand on him. Judging by her build, her own sports participation was limited to being the anchor on a tug-of-war team, but she barked at the boy, "No you can't! You ain't here to play! You're here to win!"

Poor kid. There are too many parents like that out there, in a whole range of sports, theatre, dance, whatever. They're miserable bastards who are pushing their own ambitions (often failed ones) onto their kids. I admit they're among my biggest pet peeves.

Let the kids enjoy themselves. If they're happy and learning to love what they do they'll wind up achieving much more success than all the parental shoving could ever win. And even if they don't, at least they'll have better memories to look back on than a screaming abusive parent.

.o0o.

OLD BASTARDS ARE PEOPLE, TOO

I reckon there's nothing wrong with an old bastard behaving like a big kid.

In the right kind of way, of course. Having fun, uncynical, finding the joy of life in imagination and simple things. Not the totally self-absorbed, casually cruel aspects that are also part of childhood to some extent for most if not all kids.

A mate of mine down Adelaide way has the best excuse I've heard for cutting up like a schoolboy in the first week of holidays. Apparently there'd been a few rumblings around his church – people suggesting that he didn't always "act his age". So he got up in front of the congregation one Sunday and explained.

"It's come to my attention that some of you reckon I've been behaving a bit immaturely. Not many of you are aware, I think, that I was born at five minutes to midnight on February 29th. I'll do the maths for you – earlier this year I had only my fifteenth birthday. So if it's all the same to you, yes I will act my age from time to time. And enjoy it. And anyone who wants to join me is quite welcome!"

Well said, I reckon.

*

It had been one of those days when several things were conspiring to really have me conscious of the 'Old' bit of our glorious Order's name.

I was sitting at the bar having a morose beer when I was joined by Mick - a mate who's about my vintage.

"What's up with you?" he asked me. "You look like you were out in a shower of limousines and got hit by a scooter."

I shrugged. "Aah, just had a lousy day, back's sore, working for a dropkick straight out of school who's too dumb to know how stupid he is, footpath's out there full of screaming kids… I guess I'm just feeling old."

Mick patted my shoulder consolingly. "Mate, we're not 'old'. We just share a rich cultural heritage that the young will never know."

When I stopped chuckling I felt better.

*

Deb's grandmother has been a keen gardener all her long life. She's especially fond of her roses.

She's now blind, but still tends the bushes herself as much as possible. She loves the scent while she's working, mostly by touch.

"I still enjoy my gardening," she explained, "but I meet a lot more pricks now."

*

One of my best mates in the Old Bastards has, for all the years I've known him, gone by the moniker of "Bushel". It took me a while to learn the derivation of it, but eventually one of his old drinking partners told me.

"He can be a bit of a bullshit artist," it was explained. "Some blokes, you have to take everything they say with a pinch of salt. With him, you take a bloody bushel of the stuff."

In the same vein, Crypto got his name because so often it's so hard to figure out what he's talking about, a conversation with him is like doing a cryptic crossword. It's been suggested that since he frequently doesn't know what he's on about, you can hardly expect anyone else to.

*

I heard tell recently of an old bastard who lived in a side street off a divided main road. The problem he had was that because of the median strip island he couldn't turn right into his street when driving home from work.

There was a convenient intersection nearby, controlled by a set of traffic lights. Here he could do a u-turn and get to 'his' street easily. The catch being, under local road laws, u-turns aren't permitted at traffic lights "unless otherwise signposted".

So he got himself some official looking orange safety overalls and borrowed an unmarked white utility. Then he drove around a few suburbs well away from his place until he found a "U turn Permitted" sign at a quiet intersection.

Mid-morning he parked the ute on the traffic island, as council workers do, and calmly removed the sign. Then he drove home and, in full view of the passing traffic, equally calmly attached the sign to the traffic light pole convenient to his street.

The real beauty of this story, as far as I'm concerned, is that the relocated sign stayed in place for over seven years, undisturbed by police or council. It was only when the intersection was remodeled recently that the sign was taken down. But the bracket for it is still in place, so you never know.

*

I saw a strange sight on the Sydney Harbour ferry a while back. I was sitting down the back of the boat enjoying the view, when I happened to notice a bloke pull a bottle of sherry and a small glass out of his backpack.

'Jeez, he's keen for a drink' I thought to myself as I watched him quietly pour a decent measure into the glass.

Then to my surprise he reached over the side of the ferry and tipped the measure into the harbour. After that he closed his eyes and sat quietly for a while.

Once he'd given himself a bit of a shake and put the glass and bottle back in his pack, I have to admit my curiosity got the better of me. I moved to a seat beside him and said, "Excuse me mate – I couldn't help noticing – some kind of ritual?"

The bloke grinned sheepishly and said, "Yeah, kinda. I'm from up north. When we were kids we used to come down to Sydney for holidays. Me Mum's favourite bit of the holiday was always the ferry ride over to Manly for the day. When she died we scattered her ashes in the harbour."

I nodded. "That's nice," I said.

"Mum loved her glass of sherry after tea every night," he continued. "Me or me brother get down to Sydney once or twice a year now, and every time we do we get out on the ferry and give her a drink. I reckon she'd like that we remember."

I reckon she does.

*

The fact that you're reading this pleases me - for a number of reasons. Obviously it's good for my ego, and I'm also happy about the money you paid for the book going to charities that matter a great deal to me.

I'm also very pleased by the simple fact that you can read! There are too many Australians who struggle with that, and far too many for my comfort are relatively young.

This isn't a knock on teachers, although it's disconcerting to realize quite a number of *them* can't read or write very well. There was a trendy approach to administering education a few years back that seemingly dismissed basic literacy and numeracy skills as being much less important than somehow getting kids to "find themselves".

I reckon that it'd be handy if, when they do find themselves, they could at least write a decent note.

Sometimes a lot of the blame gets put to "too much television" or more recently "too many computer games". I've got no problem with either TV or video games (other than some downright nasty gratuitously violent ones which I don't see any positive point to) as long as they don't completely replace the printed word in someone's life.

An old bastard I know – a Brit who'd had what's sometimes called "a classical education" – was rapt when his fourteen year old son came home from school with a DVD of Jane Austen's *Sense and Sensibility* that he gave every indication of really looking forward to watching.

The boy loaded himself up with a couple of 'energy drinks' and snacks and took off to his room to watch the movie. After a little while his dad decided to wander in to join him, watch along, and maybe explain some of the old-fashioned elements of Austen's classic.

When he walked in, though, to his great disappointment the TV was showing an episode of *The Simpsons*.

Picking the discarded DVD up from his son's desk he asked, "What happened to the movie?"

"It's rubbish, Dad," was the reply. "Not what I thought it was. I figured *Sense and Sensibility* was the follow up to *Dumb and Dumber*."

✱

Mac is a second generation Scot who learned the value of a quid from his father, an old Glasgow shipwright who came to Australia after the war.

Mac still remembers his twenty-first birthday, when he was at last allowed to accompany his father to the pub for his first legal beer.

Dad took him down to the local and 'introduced' him to the barman. Of course they already knew each other pretty well, and Dad knew that, but appearances had to be preserved.

"This is me lad," Dad said. "He's just turned twenty-one, ye know."

The barman looked suitably impressed. "Happy birthday, lad," he said. "I reckon this round's on the house," and poured beers for Mac and his Dad, as well as a couple of Dad's regular drinking mates who were with them.

So they sat at a table and chatted over their beers for a bit.

"Y'know Dad," said Mac, "I'm glad we can sit here and enjoy a drink together."

"Aye, well, I'm glad yer enjoyin' it son, cos it's yuir round. I got the first one remember."

*

After knocking off work early, Duncan was picking up his daughter from high school. All the way home in the car he was breaking the news to her that there'd be no television or music system when they got in.

He explained that Mum had rung earlier to say that there was a problem with the power.

They turned into their driveway, edging the car past the electricians' van already parked at the entrance.

"At least the repairman is here," commented the daughter.

"Yeah…" said Duncan as he prodded at the remote control garage door opener. "I just changed the battery in this thing…" he muttered.

A patient schoolgirl's voice came from beside him, asking, "Daddy, isn't it an *electric* motor that opens the garage door?"

*

Height is all a matter of perspective.

My dear mate Eileen was born and grew up in a very small town in Scotland. I think anyone who wasn't a local would describe it as a village.

Eileen was fairly soon the tallest in her family, and as a child was vaguely aware that her clan were pretty typical of the town.

As a teenager she went to her first inter-schools camp, where girls from across the Highlands got together for a week of Healthy Outdoor Activities. On the first day all the campers were assembled for a group photo, presumably before they'd had the chance to get too untidy.

"Right then," said the cameraman. "I want all you short ones to the front."

There was a certain amount of commotion as girls moved around. Eileen stayed where she'd stood in the middle row.

The photographer pointed to her. "You! Yes *you*. I said all the short ones to the front."

Eileen looked at him in genuine puzzlement. "But I'm not short," she said.

Standing half a head lower than the girls on either side of her didn't alter her perception one bit. To this day Eileen maintains that she has always "*thought tall*".

*

Kenneth's grand-uncle was a very traditional old Chinese gentleman. For all that he'd emigrated when he was quite young, he staunchly stuck to the old Cantonese ways.

He built up a small successful business as a market gardener, but spoke as little English as he could get away with. He preferred to deal with 'his own community'.

Over his long life he never developed much trust in the Western institution of banking. He showed no conspicuous trappings of wealth, and it was assumed he followed the old traditional practice of send any money he made, beyond his basic needs, back to China.

After the old bloke died, Kenneth was one of the family members responsible for going in to clean up the little house where he'd lived for many years. It was very Spartan in its contents, which seemed to give further weight to the idea that Grand-uncle's money had been going back across the ocean.

That was until they went to move his bed.

"It was too heavy to lift," Kenneth explained. "We realized that all the weight was in the mattress. When we tried to turn it over, this great pile of coins poured out. Some of them were Chinese coins going right back to the 1700's!"

With the little house tidied, one of Kenneth's unmarried brothers moved in.

A few months later the brother was digging in the vegetable patch in the small back yard when his spade struck metal. With only a little effort he unearthed an old coffee canister. The tin was stuffed full of banknotes, some of them decades old. It was the rest of Grand-uncle's 'savings account'.

*

A friend of mine is very reluctant to entrust her cat to her mother's care when she goes away on holiday.

"Mum's not good with animals," she reckons. "She means well, but she's so bad she's killed a glass fish."

I suggested that was an unkind exaggeration but apparently it's not.

Mum at one point had a little tank with some ornamental fish made of coloured glass floating in it. She somehow let all the water in the tank evaporate. When that was finally noticed, the fish were discovered upside down on the bottom of the aquarium, most of them cracked after having been allowed to dry out completely.

I reckon I wouldn't trust her with a real animal either. Even a pet rock would be a chance of running away.

*

I heard this story from Jean, who was a census taker in the UK back in the 1970's. They had a very different system to the one we're used to in Australia. Instead of filling in a form yourself, you were interviewed by the census taker.

This brave soul went from door to door, doing a quick interview with whoever was home to get the basic details of who lived there, how old they were, where they were born, and what they did for a crust.

Jean called at the door of a house in a slightly-smaller-than-medium town, and was met by a harried looking woman trailing six kids aged from about six months to seven years. In the course of the interview the woman made a passing remark about her husband having died four years earlier.

Jean looked at the brood and said "Sorry – perhaps I misunderstood. Did you say your husband died four years ago?"

"That's right," nodded the woman, who then caught Jean's drift and added, "He died. I didn't."

*

Wazza had just brought his new girlfriend back to his flat for the first time. She glanced into the bedroom as they walked past on their way to the lounge.

"Oh," she said disappointedly. "I see you leave your clothes all over the floor. I guess you can't be bothered hanging them up or putting them away."

"Oh no, it's not that," replied Wazza airily. "I just always wanted a carpeted wardrobe."

*

Kari's a tall attractive girl who knows just how good her legs are. She often dresses to show them off and isn't averse to genuine appreciative comments.

She has her standards though, and was particularly unimpressed with one sweaty old bastard she encountered in the mall. She was wearing a very short skirt, and he was calling out for her to bend over for him.

"Just two inches will do! Bend over two inches!" he yelled, trying to amuse or impress his mates.

After yet another "Just two inches!" Kali turned on him and said loudly, "Mate, if all you can offer is just two inches you're getting nothing from me, or anyone else I reckon!"

That shut him up, amidst the laughter of his mates.

*

Sometimes it's all a matter of timing.

I was meeting Gill in a city pub after work. She'd gotten there before me and was buying herself a drink as I walked in. She hadn't spotted me so I went to the bar to get my own beer as she walked away to a booth.

I admit to being biased, but she looked good in jeans and a top that showed off her figure to best advantage. A little ferret-like character at the bar beside me had also been admiring her.

"Nice body on that, eh?" he said none too quietly, with a sly grin on his face.

"Yep," I replied, just as audibly. "That's one of the reasons I married her."

The bloke went very pale, and Gill's smile was bright enough to read by.

*

For a while I worked with an amazingly conceited young woman we'll call Narelle. She came from a very well-off background – South Australian 'old money'. Narelle was "upper class" and was more aware of that than anyone I'd ever met.

Any bloke who had any ideas of going out with her had to be prepared to have his pedigree examined in detail. His income, current and potential, made up a significant part of the 'acceptability' equation, but ultimately the final criterion was his bloodline.

Given that Narelle was pretty cute there were quite a few guys who, over time, tried their luck with her. To give her her due she allowed them to lavish their affections on her, at least until they'd been grilled as to their ancestry. And believe me, claims were checked. As I understand it Narelle's family were as big on this as she was, if not bigger.

One of the unpleasant aspects of this was the way anyone who 'failed the test' was treated. It was bad enough if you just worked with Narelle and came from a lower class background (and most people did) – she would just talk down to you.

The blokes who'd gone out with but were subsequently discarded had it even worse. They were hardly spoken to at all. Now that might not seem like much of a loss, but for any guy working with her who was in that category, it was difficult, uncomfortable and often downright embarrassing.

I said Narelle was more class conscious than anyone I'd ever met. That changed when eventually our team was joined by Pablo.

He was the descendant of Andalucian nobility or some such rot. His European old money was more than a match for Narelle's South Aussie non-convict stock. Pablo seemed to walk about with his long patrician nose so far in the air it was amazing he didn't collide with every desk in the place.

Inevitably Pablo and Narelle clashed at first. Egos like theirs – how could they co-exist? Equally inevitably, perhaps, they became An Item. What seemed to us outsiders a remarkable thing happened. Pablo passed the pedigree test and suddenly Narelle put her own ego on the back burner.

She became no less conceited, but now the conceit was based on Pablo and his sterling qualities. Most of these were lost on the rest of us. Before long they announced their forthcoming wedding. None of us workmates were invited to the actual ceremony, far less the reception, although I think the most senior of managers may have been asked along.

We were told the date, time and address of the Event if we wished to stand outside and watch the happy couple emerge from the ceremony. I jokingly asked one of my colleagues if he was planning to attend.

"I'm tempted to," he replied. "It's such a happy occasion, after all."

I looked at him skeptically. "Give me a break," I said. "You're no more fond of Narelle and Pablo than I am. What's so 'happy' about it?"

The old bastard smiled at me and said, "Just think. Them getting married to each other has saved two other people from a lifetime of misery."

*

Sometimes relationships just don't work out, unfortunately. I overheard a woman in a café grumbling to a friend, "The only thing my husband and I have in common is an anniversary on the same day."

My first marriage wasn't that bad, but it did go beyond its 'use-by date'. After it was over I spent a while enjoying being single before I met up with Gill while I was working in Adelaide. I'll spare you the details, but as you might surmise from the dedication at the start of this book, things worked out well for us and we shared a lot of great years.

A couple of years into the relationship we decided to get married and happily shared the news with our friends. We got lots of support and enthusiasm, even though some of my mates who remembered my earlier effort at matrimonial bliss were a bit more cautious.

My great mate Rosco summed up nicely: "A second marriage, eh? That's the triumph of hope over experience."

I'm pleased to report that Rosco was best man when I married Meredith – my second triumph of hope!

*

There was a song a while back that included the line "people in love do funny things". It's true, you know.

George in Canberra was asked by his boss to go to north Queensland to work for a couple of months. Not too hard to take, you might think, and in many ways you'd be right. The problem for George however was that his girlfriend Cathy couldn't go with him. She couldn't get that much time off work, it was made clear to George that he'd been 'asked' to travel in the sense that refusal would be regarded as a notice of resignation, and neither of them could afford to lose their jobs.

When the day of their tearful parting at the airport came, George kept asking, "What can I send you back? I want to send you something."

"Lots of postcards will do, darling," Cathy replied

"I want to send you a gift."

"No, really. I just want you to come back – as soon as you can."

"But I want to send you something tropical," George kept on, regardless of Cathy's protests.

Finally in exasperation she said, "Oh, just send me a coconut or something!"

George smiled and was content. They exchanged a few more romantic minutes before he boarded his plane and headed north.

A couple of weeks later Cathy got a note asking her to collect a package from her local Post Office. She brought the package in to work with her next day.

It was her coconut. Her address was written on the hard outer shell in thick black marking pen, with "Love from George xxx" on the reverse.

Obviously the glue on postage stamps didn't take to coconut shell very effectively – he'd used a staple gun to attach four stamps to the nut. I don't know what impressed me more – George's ingenuity or Australia Post's willingness to deliver his romantic gesture.

*

I can only wonder at the devotion of some couples, or the individuals in them. Sometimes it seems in complete defiance of common sense.

Bushel had been having a few beers and a lot of chat with Mullet, Ted and some of the boys, when he decided he ought to head home and get a few things done there. So he rang his girlfriend of the time and asked her to drive over and pick him up outside the pub in ten minutes. She quite happily agreed to this.

"Be right with you then, dear," Bushel said. "Ten minutes," he said after hanging up. "Plenty of time for another one."

Of course he got talking again – he could talk under wet cement with a few drinks in him. 'Another one' turned into another four before Mullet said, "Weren't you getting picked up to go home?"

"Oh, that's right," said Bushel and casually wandered over to the door. There was no car park handy and sure enough, there was his girlfriend, dutifully driving round and round the block waiting for him to emerge.

On the other side of the coin, I was walking through a department store once when I noticed a bloke sitting on a little plastic chair near the changing room in the ladies wear section. Having made eye contact we nodded a wordless greeting to each other.

Returning an hour later after visiting several other shops I noticed he was on the same chair.

"Back again, or still here?" I asked with a grin.

"Still here," he replied with a tired smile.

"Why don't you go grab a cup of coffee or something and just agree to meet up later?" I asked.

"No, mate. Nice idea, but she likes to come out and get me opinion every so often."

"Fair enough, I suppose," I said. "Does it make any difference?"

"Doesn't seem to," he shrugged, "but it makes her happy."

Actually, it does make a difference in some cases. JB's been happily married for nigh on twenty years. He reckons he's learned the secret of going clothes shopping with his wife Penny.

"If I sound enthusiastic about something she tries on, she won't buy it," he explained. "She figures I must like it 'cause it's revealing and shows off her body."

Penny, I must point out, is a good-looking attractively built woman. JB reckons she's very self-conscious though, so won't wear anything that she thinks might attract too much attention.

"I get it," I said. "If you want her to buy something, you just say you don't like it."

"Nah – that doesn't work. She worries that I might be right and it *doesn't* look good on her."

"So you can't win?"

"Not necessarily. If I'm serious about her getting something good I take her Mum out with us. She's a fly old bugger. We get on well, and if I give her the quiet nod she'll sell Penny on the gear."

*

Len's one of those blokes who's perhaps too bright for his own good. He gets bored easily and creates his own amusement. He's sometimes kindly described as eccentric.

When he fitted spotlights to his car he made up a little nameplate to attach to the dashboard control switch. On this was engraved 'Death Ray'.

To enhance the effect he bought one of those little 'sound effects' key rings from a good toy shop. He then rigged it so that turning on the spotlights activated a short burst of ray gun noise.

Actually, given the effect the spotlights had on wildlife on his local country roads – immobilizing animals before they cannoned off his bull bar – the term 'Death Ray' was probably pretty right.

*

The interior of the little local church hall Len's mother attended was badly in need of a coat of paint. To keep the peace at home Len agreed to do the job, at no cost of course.

At one point during the job it occurred to him that he was using the same size and style of brush that Rolf Harris used.

For those not old enough to remember Rolf's old variety shows on television, I'll explain. The shows often included a segment where Rolf would whip up a nifty landscape or portrait using only a couple of colours, a wide house-painting brush and a big piece of plain board. And he'd do it in quick time while chatting to the audience or a guest on the program who might be the subject of the portrait.

So, inspired by the memory of Rolf's work, Len whipped up a quick portrait of Mr. Harris in white paint on the wall of the church.

After admiring his handiwork for a few moments, he dutifully went about completing his more mundane task. This of course included painting over his portrait.

The job was done, and Len's mother was suitably pleased. All seemed well.

Then on the following Sunday a strange thing happened. As the sun beamed through one of the eastern windows of the church hall it shone along the north wall. The glancing rays cast shadows from the slight irregularities in the surface where Len had painted over his Rolf Harris portrait.

Before the astonished eyes of the congregation a face gradually became visible. Try telling a group of dedicated church-goers that a bearded face miraculously appearing on their wall is really Rolf Harris, not a vision of The Lord!

*

Len's always regarded himself as being good with animals. He reckons there's only one time when he's ever been tempted to do deliberate harm to an animal.

He and his girlfriend were indulging in some 'afternoon delight' in his room one Saturday. The young lady in question was apparently particularly noisy in her enthusiasm.

Unbeknownst to either of them, Len's cat Spike had been sleeping on top of the wardrobe, until the girl's shrieks and cries woke him.

Disturbed, Spike jumped down from the wardrobe to seek a quieter resting place. Unfortunately, the spot on the bed where Spike normally landed was presently occupied by Len's bare buttocks.

Spike landed, claws extended. Len hollered and reacted so violently that the bed collapsed. The girlfriend, who'd been under Len at the time, screamed with unalloyed delight.

Spike beat a hasty retreat. Len struggled to his feet, trying to stem the bleeding from his punctured posterior.

"What about the girl?" I asked as he recounted the incident.

"Silly cow asked if we could do that again. Cattus interruptus, I call it," he grumbled.

*

Trev has a very responsible job high up in the PNG bureaucracy these days, but when he was younger he was a serious drinker. He's tall and skinny, but gave every indication of having hollow legs that he could store beer in. And with a few ales in him he was prone to acting on sudden impulse with little apparent thought about consequences.

I remember a Wednesday evening when he and I went out for a couple of quiet drinks after work. By about two in the morning we'd wandered in an out of most of the bars and clubs in town.

Suddenly he announced, "I want to go to the Moose!"

"Um… I don't think you're dressed for it," I tried to suggest, but Trev would have none of that, and off we went.

Here I should explain that the Moose was the local bikers' bar and Trev, having come straight from his managerial job, was still wandering about in business slacks, tweed jacket, no-longer-quite-so-crisp white shirt, and an inch-wide wool tie. Having a rather lower-profile job and a clear idea of my place in the career hierarchy, I was in my usual jeans and black t-shirt, and thus felt appropriately attired for the Moose.

As we walked in the bar went a bit quiet. Not menacingly silent, but there was no doubt we were Noticed. Oblivious, Trev arranged his lanky frame on a stool at the bar and ordered us a couple of beers.

The beers were served. 'So far so good' I thought to myself, and started to relax. At which point Trev accosted a bloke walking past on his way back from the Men's.

"See here my man! That's a terribly scruffy jacket you have on!" he said, indicating the bloke's (admittedly very battered and worn) leathers. He continued to berate the bemused biker, even jabbing his long bony finger into the guy's shoulder.

Trev's over six feet tall, but has the physique of a pipe cleaner. The biker, or any of his mates, could have broken him into bits in less time than it takes you to read this. Amazingly that didn't happen.

The biker, unable to get a word in, looked past Trev at me. I gave him what I hoped was an apologetic smile, shrugged, pointed at Trev's glass then tapped the side of my head.

'Turns into an imbecile when drunk' was what I was hoping to communicate. It seemed to work. The bloke nodded, his mates relaxed back into their chairs, and when Trev finally stopped for breath the biker patted him on the shoulder and said, "Yair. Right. Thanks pal."

Trev turned back to the bar, then nodded vaguely at me and said, "See, you just have to know how to speak to people."

*

Whatever else Trev's failings, he wouldn't drive when drunk. Not knowingly, anyway.

There were several occasions though, when he'd have 'a couple' after work and then go to drive home. What usually happened was that he'd soon realize that he wasn't sober enough to drive after all. He'd pull over, park the car at the side of the road, then hail a taxi to either take him home or, more usually, back to the pub.

There was more than one instance of Trev arriving at work the next morning and plaintively asking if anyone "knew where he'd left the car last night?"

Sometimes a search party would have to be mounted. We'd drive along the approximate route that Trev should have taken to get home. The key word here is 'should'. The trouble was, one of the things that would indicate to Trev that he shouldn't be driving was the sudden realization that he was lost.

Once, three days searching had failed to turn up the car. It looked like time to call in the police. Trev was always reluctant to do this, as explaining the car's loss would almost certainly involve admitting he'd been Driving Under The Influence.

By luck a friend who lived on the outskirts of town chanced upon the car. It was nearly an hour's drive in exactly the opposite direction to that which Trev should have been going.

*

When he first started working in Canberra Trev tried to cultivate an image of conservatism, even naiveté, which was at serious variance to his fondness for a drink.

One evening a few of the boys were bragging about real or imagined sexual conquests. His face a picture of wide-eyed innocence Trev said, "Oh, I've never had one of those."

Fueled by the drinks, Alan announced that the group should remedy that sad state of affairs. Mick and Ross were roped in, and Alan led the way to a little upstairs brothel he "happened to have heard about".

That explanation soon lost credibility when it was noticed that the madam of the brothel knew Alan by name. Alan explained to her that the purpose of the visit was to introduce 'young Trevor' to the ways of the world.

So the 'guest of honour' was given first pick of the available girls. Alan swiftly made his choice, and followed Trev and his companion through the curtains into the back rooms.

Mick was by far the least sober of the group, and I think that the madam realized that all he would do if led to a horizontal position would be pass out. Recognizing that he'd be a difficult dead weight to shift she decided the best thing to do with him was to steer him towards the exit door.

Right about this time, Ross' parsimonious nature kicked in. He decided that, being none to keen on paying the prices expected for his own gratification, he certainly wasn't going to help bankroll Trev's. With some reluctance he took custody of Mick and led the way to a cab rank.

Alan emerged a little while later and upon discovering that Ross and Mick had already left, quickly paid his own bill and slipped away.

When Trev finally finished enjoying his 'treat' he found he'd been left to pay for his own pleasure after all.

I can't say I was all that sympathetic when I heard the story. I'd known Trev before he came to Canberra, and was pretty sure he'd have been taking the boys' charity under false pretences anyway.

*

I used to work for a woman who was (inaccurately) rumoured to have earlier worked as a prostitute in Sydney. She was quite happy to play up to the fiction. Initially she picked up the nickname Crossply, alluding to her mythical days on Kings Cross, plying her trade.

Upon hearing this her husband Bob shook his head. "Nah," he said, playing along. "That was a long time ago. These days she's a Retread."

He really did play up to his wife's putative 'dark past'. Bob and Retread worked on different floors of the same building. One morning they were sharing a crowded lift. Arriving at Bob's floor he turned to her, handed over a $20 note, said, "That's for last night," and stepped out nimbly just as the doors closed.

Caught completely off guard, Retread looked around the crowd of unfamiliar faces – a few grinning, some trying to look in any direction but at her. She reckoned that the journey up the next few floors felt like it took an hour. She told me, "I tried saying 'He's my husband – really' but it didn't seem to help!"

*

There's a bloke I know working in an office over on the other side of town. We'll call him Donald. He's a tedious snob who's got a number of unpleasant and unoriginal nicknames, although I must admit I like Woodworm (he could bore a hole in a timber desk).

In the same office is a lady Old Bastard who Woodworm really can't stand. He's so rude he'll just turn his back and walk away whenever she comes near him. He's told people that he considers her so intellectually inferior that he can't abide her presence. I reckon that's more than a bit harsh.

She looks out for the rest of the staff. If she spots anyone looking really bothered by having Woodworm bend their ear about his favourite subject (himself), she'll wander over just to say "G'day". It's guaranteed he'll take off pretty much right away. It's won her the affection of her colleagues, and the nickname of Mortein because she's such a good pest repellent!

*

It was common amongst one group of blokes I knew to describe anyone who was a right dill as having two <*gentleman's appendages*> because he couldn't get that silly just playing with one.

The saddest case we worked with was a guy <u>so</u> infuriatingly, maybe willfully, dense that he was known to all in the team as "Ninety-nine". It had nothing to do with Barbara Feldon in *Get Smart*.

*

One of the blokes I used to play football alongside was incredibly accident prone. He'd trip over his bootlaces, collide with a goalpost, tread on a moving ball and go flying.

He risked injury just getting out of the car when he arrived at the game. He wasn't just a disaster area waiting to happen - he was known to all of us as "Holocaust".

*

Years ago I knew a bloke who had a dead set mania for giving others nicknames. Possibly because he'd been christened Harry he was determined that all his mates would have '---y' names.

There was 'Kenny', who wasn't a Ken at all, but bore a passing resemblance to the kids' character Kenny Koala. Tom got the slightly inappropriate nickname of 'Ugly'. His younger brother got 'Little Ugly' or more usually 'Ug'.

It was Harry who was responsible for me carrying the moniker of 'Paddy' for years (to my initial irritation though I got used to it) on the basis that he couldn't tell an Irish accent from the Scots accent I spoke with at the time.

Paul Comerford hung around with us for a while. Harry quickly dubbed him 'Comby', or 'Kombi'. The rest of us soon morphed that into 'VW'.

With all the '---y' nicknames going around, getting introduced to us must have been like stumbling into a meeting of the seven dwarfs.

*

Oskie was a serious drinker. He got his nickname from his habit, when in his cups (which was often), of climbing onto a table or bar and bellowing what he reckoned was an old war cry of an Indian tribe back in Canada.

Nobody, including I suspect the man himself, knew exactly how the war cry went, far less *what* it meant. But it sounded like "Oskie-wah-wah!" It was often the last thing you'd hear from him before he was required to Leave The Premises.

Oskie was a big bloke who kept getting bigger. Remarkably, he was only ever known to drink Diet Lager. Mind you, he was known to knock off a six-pack or two before breakfast on occasion. It was suggested that if he drank 'normal' beer as much, or as long, he'd have needed his own postcode.

*

Standing at a bar in Chiltern, I was watching the races on telly with a few folks I'd met there. Another of their mates came in and joined us.

I couldn't help but notice he had really badly crossed eyes. How he could see well enough to even walk in a straight line I honestly don't know.

He was introduced to me as 'Bloodhound'.

"It's me eyes," he explained. "While one of 'em is lookin' *at* ya, the other one is lookin' *for* ya."

*

During the CB radio craze of the late '70's a lot of people were giving themselves call signs. Some were dull, some were witty, and some were downright delusional.

Dutch and I were driving around the western suburbs of Brisbane one night. Flicking around on his CB radio we chanced on an especially attractive-sounding female voice. 'Maria21' or something disappointingly uninspired like that, she called herself.

The other half of the conversation was a guy who sounded like a sixteen year old still anxiously awaiting puberty, but unsubtly calling himself 'Footlong'. He did *not* sound like Joel Garner.

Dutch and I listened in amusement as Footlong made more and more of a pest of himself, trying to arrange a face-to-face with Maria21 so he could "make it with her".

Finally in serious irritation the girl said "Listen, loser, I'd rather make it with a cucumber than you!"

At which point a new voice cut in. "Breaker breaker – this is the cucumber…"

*

One of the local cricket teams evidently has a few blokes in the side with some classical education.

They disdainfully christened their wicket keeper "Coleridge", inspired by *The Rime Of The Ancient Mariner*.

Apparently the hapless glove man could only 'stoppeth one of three'.

*

Two of my absolute best mates are Marianne and Don. They're uncomplicated, good hearted, loyal and loving. They're also just about the most devoted couple I've had the pleasure to know.

They both realize that they're the best thing to ever happen to each other. Whichever of them is writing to you the letter, card or e-mail would always be signed "*Marianne and Don*".

Eventually they twigged that if they just used the initials we'd all know who the mail was from, not least because of how appropriate they are. Like I said, two of the loveliest people I know, and by their own admission silly as two bob watches. So it's entirely appropriate when they introduce themselves to someone by saying, "G'day. We're MAD."

*

Back in the pre-computerised days of the Public Service all departments ran on complex paper systems. There was a file for everything and all the files had to be accounted for.

In the Tax Office there was a big index system that tracked where things were. The official job title of the people who actually did the tracking of files and documents was "Searcher" and a degree of creative thinking and stubbornness were valuable personality traits to have.

The people who actually worked on the correspondence and tax returns themselves each had a unique seven letter code assigned to them. That was recorded on the index system for every file every time it moved through the steps of processing, so it was theoretically possible for a Searcher to locate any file at any time.

The first four letters of the code identified the section that the employee worked in, and the last three were their initials.

My old mate Dave had a code something like SECB:DDL. The DDL prompted the nickname 'Diddles'. It was so delightfully inappropriate for a big husky Mediterranean type like Dave that of course it stuck.

Mind you, I think some members of the public may have been disturbed to find their tax returns were being assessed by a bloke known as 'Diddles'.

*

Kev's been retired from the commercial traveller caper for a few years now. He used to be the rep for several companies – a few of them at the same time, I suspect. He clocked up so many miles travelling around Australia that he reckons he may as well have gone to the moon and back twice.

The travel bug obviously got deep under Kev's skin, though, because retirement hasn't done much to curtail his wandering. He's now very much a part of that mob commonly called 'Grey Nomads'. They're the 60+ brigade who routinely trek between caravan parks, campsites and affordable motels right across the country.

Some do it to keep finding new experiences. Others are the opposite, constantly revisiting old haunts and old friends.

Kev is pretty much in that second category. There probably aren't many places left in Australia that he *hasn't* visited. And he's fancied himself a ladies' man all his life. I think his 'little black book' is a four volume set.

The trouble is, age and a life on the road haven't been kind to Kev. He doesn't cut the dashing figure he did in his working days, especially the early ones.

Apparently quite a few of his past 'conquests' have been more than a bit disappointed at the grey and saggy old bastard who's turned up on their doorstep after an absence of years.

So much so that his mates have nicknamed him The Fireman – he goes around the country putting out old flames.

*

Mick was reminiscing about his much-missed old pal Chugga.

"He often used to say: life's funny, then you die. And so he did."

But Chugga, Mick and I all agreed – if it's not then you're not doing it right.

*

Three things to ponder:

If everyone ran away from their problems, would we at least all be running in the same direction for a change?

Research is costly but outcomes are priceless.

Experience is only valuable if you learn from it.

.o0o.

THE BASTARD HAS A DRINK

A sunny afternoon at The Rocks – we've wandered out into the courtyard behind one of the fine old pubs there.

There were some nice old trees, a few tubs of flowers, and a big sign that read "Welcome To Our Beer Garden".

Cheery Old Bastard KJ sees the sign, smiles broadly and says, "Ah! So this is where they grow beer!"

*

There were a few of us sitting at a table in the Observer Hotel. Thal wandered over to join us.

He was carefully carrying three large beers. That seemed a little odd, only because as far as we knew Thal wasn't in a round with anyone.

"You got a big thirst up, mate?" asked Michael.

Thal shrugged, indicated the beers and replied, "My doctor reckons I need glasses."

*

We were having a morning session one public holiday. They're something of a rare treat for those in the workforce, especially those with busy weekends. So there were a few of us making the most of the opportunity this day.

We hadn't been at the bar all that long when Johnno had to go and relieve himself.

"Just going to shake hands with the wife's best friend," he explained.

"Shake hands with the unemployed more like it," was a response from someone who wasn't his wife.

Soon after Johnno resumed his place at the bar, looking rather more comfortable.

"The first leak of the day – it's like virginity. Once it's gone you can't get it back," he observed sagely.

Shaz didn't even look up from her beer as she replied, "Actually, you can get surgery these days…"

Those of us with vivid imaginations found our eyes watering or glazing over. Or both.

Steve decided to let that one go through to the keeper. Instead he decided to take a leaf out of Johnno's book and go relieve himself.

As he got up he remarked, "I like frequent visits to the toilet when I'm drinking. It reminds me I can still walk."

*

I was chatting to a bloke in Scotland who'd not long retired from a long career as a civil engineer. (I'm pleased to report he was still a very civil gentleman.)

He related a story from early in his working life, when he was doing a job for a few days in one of the great distilleries on Islay.

At that time, all the workers would be given a wee dram at noon with their lunch, and another at three to get them through the afternoon. As he was working on-site he was invited to join them.

He duly took his place in the queue, under the watchful eye of a Customs & Excise officer whose job it was to account for every drop of alcohol. The chap serving dipped his ladle into the government-approved serving vessel, and poured a dram into the engineer's ceramic mug.

"Och, whatever ye do, don't sip it!" came the warning, a fraction too late.

As my friend describes it, it was like one of those sitcom moments when the character is changing colour and frantically moving their mouth with no sound coming out.

The pourer thrust a milk bottle full of water into the engineer's hand with the instruction "Quick, drink this!"

It hadn't been the nice drop of ten-year-old or better single malt that he'd been expecting. Instead, it was the stuff that's yet to be aged inside a cask – 'first spirit' it's called, interestingly flavoured, quite clear, and at least 67% alcohol. To be swallowed in one go, not sipped at delicately.

No wonder it was restricted to one wee dram at a time!

*

I was walking along one of Brisbane's city streets on a Saturday afternoon. Half a dozen twenty-something year old lasses walked past in the opposite direction, or more accurately, staggered.

Clearly they'd been having a few cold ones at one of the pubs up the road. Well, it was a typically humid Brisbane day so I couldn't blame them.

One of the girls was particularly the worse for wear, and there was an unfortunate and unattractive line of drool running down her chin.

Very considerately I thought, one of her mates reached over with a tissue as they walked and wiped the sticky wet trail off. The sense of care and concern was somewhat diminished when the friend loudly said, "Oh wow – you must be, like, sweating from your mouth!"

*

I picked up this story from the Tamar Valley in northern Tasmania.

Some quite well-off locals had a wine cellar under their house, with a lot of good stuff in it, both local and imported.

Of course, there was some not-so-expensive stuff too. They were the casual 'drink whenever' bottles that were to be opened with dinner. Not rubbish, but not quite what they thought of as 'special occasion' wine.

But then there was a bad storm, and a lot of rain. The cellar flooded, but it took the owners a few days to realise it.

When they did discover the damage, the water level was half way up the cellar wall. And floating on the surface of the water: a layer of wine labels that had come adrift from their bottles.

From then on, it was like a magical mystery tour. Beyond the basic question of red, white or bubbles, the only way to identify the majority of their wine collection was to drink it.

The nice thing about this is that they wisely took the attitude that it made every occasion a 'special occasion'.

I reckon it's the wine drinking equivalent of treating every day as if it were your last.

*

A conversation about old style dance bands and the venues they play in brought up an interesting term for certain clubs on Queensland's Gold Coast: "silver scrotum clubs'.

So named because they're places that hold old peoples balls.

*

A few interesting cocktail recipes I've picked up around the world (some worth knowing just for the name!):

Something Wicked This Way Comes: Fresh strawberries muddled with mint, Polish bison-grass vodka, raspberry coulis and lemon vodka – shaken with crushed ice, served in a glass with an icing sugar rim.

Keith Richards: Green faery absinthe, Benedictine and orange juice.

Sexual Misconduct With Freckles: piolunowka absinthe with champagne

Gold Digger: Goldwasser, vanilla vodka and whisky.

Pleasant Street Tea: Turkish apple tea, pomegranate molasses and honey vodka

Lockwood martini: Belvedere vodka martini with a splash of sparkling moscato & 2 raspberries. Served with Australian Lavender Cove oysters at Chicago's Palmer Hotel (which was once the world's biggest, and is still amongst the most opulent!)

.oOo.

THE OLD BASTARD ON THE ROAD

Over the years I've spent a lot of time driving. Some of it was for work, a lot of it was, and is, for pleasure. Australia's a big place (and part of an even bigger planet – more of that later) and I admit I just don't understand people who've got no interest in seeing anything outside their own little bit of it.

Some years back I met a couple of young blokes who were driving up the east coast of the country. Whenever they ran out of money (which apparently was fairly often) they'd drop anchor and pick up whatever work they could find – picking fruit, builders' labourers, deckhands on trawlers or cruise boats.

Mick and Oyster had figured they'd be doing it tough for a fair bit of the time, so they'd worked out ways of travelling and living cheap. The most obvious one was to sleep in the car whenever possible. The catch was that in order to cut costs further, they'd got the cheapest, most economical car they could find: a Fiat Bambino.

If you've never seen one, they're not much bigger than an upturned bathtub with wheels. To avoid arguments Mick and Oyster kept all of their luggage, such as it was, on the back seat, and each slept in one of the tiny front seats. The things some bastards do for mateship.

*

There were four of us working up along the central coast of Queensland. Three of us were, relatively speaking, old hands, but Geoff was a new boy. And still a bit prone to letting his enthusiasm get in the way of his common sense.

Among the things he was enthusiastic about were cars. His own was a beat-up old Holden, so when we'd scored a you-beaut brand new top of the range model as our hire car for the central coast trip he was as happy as a dog with two tails. Especially with all the extra fittings and trimmings and gadgets the car came equipped with.

We were belting along the Bruce Highway at what I'll diplomatically call *about* 100kph. Geoff was sitting in the front passenger seat, still exploring the various switches and dials within his reach. He popped open the glove box and discovered yet another button.

Now, a brighter bastard might have taken a clue from the fact that this was, unlike nearly all of the other buttons in the car, a red button.

The fateful phrase. "I wonder what this button does," said Geoff, and before anyone could stop him he pressed it.

It was the boot lock.

The boot lid flew open, and at 100+ kilometres per hour we watched out the back window as our luggage flew and bounced in our wake. The only person not looking out behind us was Geoff, who was still peering into the glove box to see what the button had done.

As we drove back down the highway picking up our debris, there was much heated discussion around the idea that Geoff should have been sent back on foot to collect everything. I think all that saved him from that fate or worse was that none of the cartons of beer in the boot had been amongst the items to take flight.

*

I'll preface this next story by making it clear that I am NOT endorsing or encouraging drunk driving. I freely admit it's something I got away with more often than I should have in younger and stupider days.

It was a time, perhaps a generation, when getting behind the wheel after a few beers (or more) was just accepted as something a lot of blokes did. Getting booked was something that happened to other people, but was still a more serious consideration than the prospect of actually being hurt or killed, or hurting/killing anyone else. Now, I hope, most of us know better.

Certainly it dawned on me how lucky I'd been after a couple of very close escapes, and after a few people I knew weren't so lucky.

All of that said, I really can't leave this one out of a chapter about bastards on the road. The bastard in question was coach of a football team I was in at the time. On this particular chilly, damp day we'd copped a flogging in our morning match, then retired to the Pineapple Hotel (near the Gabba in Brisbane) to console ourselves over a lot of beers.

A few hours later four of us stumbled out to Coach's battered old Holden. He'd driven us to the game, so it was naturally assumed he'd drive us home. We were aware he'd had a few drinks, but so had we. In fact we'd had enough to not realize just how far gone Coach really was.

That was, until the Holden was pulled over by a motorcycle policeman who indicated that Coach was "driving erratically".
"Step out of the car, please, sir," said the copper, as he opened the driver's door.

'Step' is the wrong word. Without the door to prop him up Coach toppled sideways, seemingly in slow motion, out onto the road at the cop's feet, where he giggled and burped. The policeman's eyes lit up at the thickness of the book he was about to throw.

Just as he got his pen out of his pocket though, the radio on his bike went off. Apparently there was a Major Disturbance somewhere nearby that he was urgently required to attend. He leaned into the car and looked at the four of us.
"Can any of you drive?" he asked.
"Um… yeah…" ventured one or two nervous voices.
"Right," said the copper, "Get yourselves and… *that* (indicating Coach) out of here." Then he jumped back on his bike and sped off.

With some difficulties we got Coach back on his feet. One of the biggest difficulties was that none of us could stand very well by this point, either. On what we blearily thought was the sound principle that he knew the tricks to starting his cantankerous old car and we didn't, we re-inserted him into the driver's seat. With exaggerated caution Coach weaved our way home. Safe, but definitely more by luck than good judgement!

*

The main highways around Australia are, on the whole, pretty good. You get a few rough spots but when you consider the volume of heavy vehicles that trundle around, and how remote some of the stretches of road are from regular maintenance crews, we do alright.

Once you get off the 'major' roads though, things can get a bit rough. I've been on some that really are tough on a car.

I reckon the single worst I've traveled was the way out from Woomera into the opal fields of the Great Stony Desert. Trust me – that place is well named. Once we got off the sealed section of road the little Ford Laser we were in started to really rattle on the rocks. Inside, we bounced and shook like dice in a cup while Neale the driver belted along at high speed.

After a while of this Rosco, who was sitting in the back of the car, tapped Neale on the shoulder.

"There's a funny noise coming from somewhere under the car," he said.

Neale and I couldn't hear a thing, as Neale had cranked the volume of the cassette player up to nearly maximum in a vain effort to drown out the rattle of stones and metalwork.

"Are you sure?" I asked. "I mean, how would you tell?"

Rosco looked worried. "I can feel it coming up through the floor," he replied.

Neale shrugged and stopped the car. There was no point in 'pulling over' – the road was a roughly graded strip barely discernible from the surrounding desert. As much for the sake of stretching our legs as anything, we all got out to walk around and inspect the car.

It wasn't difficult to spot the problem. Some time earlier we must have blown one of the rear tyres on a sharp rock, but nobody had heard it happen.

It must have been quite a while back though, because the tyre had been progressively disintegrating. By now the rubber had completely gone. What Rosco had heard, or felt, was the wheel rim clattering against the stones. Even the rim was starting to crack and chip. We were lucky to be able to get the spare tyre on and continue, at a rather more sedate pace!

*

The road from Yulara out to the Olgas is, under normal circumstances, a reasonable one. After heavy rain, though, it's a bit more challenging.

I was out there in such conditions several years ago. I'd taken Rosco on holiday with me from Canberra to see the sights of Central Australia. Being a Tasmanian on his first big journey inland it was all an adventure for the old bastard. At one point along the Stuart Highway I noticed he'd gone very quiet.

"What's up?" I asked him.

"It's just occurred to me," he replied, "I've never been this far from the ocean before."

It had rained solidly for several days before we got to Alice Springs, so the area looked very different to what I'd encountered on a previous trip, and what you usually see in pictures. To this day I don't think Rosco is 100% convinced that the Todd River doesn't normally have water in it. But having travelled all that way we weren't going to let a bit of water on the road deter us.

Perhaps sensibly we should have, given that we weren't in any sort of conventional off-road vehicle. We'd done the trip in 'Bernadette' – my trusty old Holden Commodore.

We'd had a good run on our first day out from the Uluru 'resort' at Yulara out to Ayers Rock. (I'm happy to talk about Uluru National Park with all due respect, but I grew up calling the big lump of rock sticking out of the middle of it by the old explorers' name – that's *my* tradition.)

The Rock looks spectacular in the rain, by the way. The running water takes off the top layer of orange, which is effectively rust, I'm told, and the whole thing takes on an elegant silver sheen. If it looked like this all the time I guess it wouldn't seem as effective, but the contrast to your 'expected' view is really striking.

So on day two of our visit, undaunted by more overnight rain, we drove off to see the Olgas. In fact it had turned out to be quite a fine sunny day, so I was a little surprised the first time I encountered water over the road.

That perhaps understates it a little. We appeared to have come to the intersection of the road and something like a creek. This was apparently such an unusual phenomenon that there was no depth indicator. Or as Rosco pointed out perhaps it had washed away.

Certainly he was none too impressed when I asked him to get out and check the depth of the water.

"What with?" he asked with some force.

"Oh I don't know – find a long stick or a branch or something," I suggested.

"Look around you idiot!" was the reply. "We're in the desert. Well, it's usually a desert. Do you see any trees providing handy long poles?"

I conceded that he had a point. My next suggestion – that he wade out into the stream to see how deep it was – was even less well received.

"Oh well, I'll just have to risk it then," I said. I cranked up the volume of the Beach Boys 'Surfin' USA' cassette and planted my foot on the accelerator. I held Bernadette steady, kept up a nice constant not-too-fast not-too-slow speed, and comfortably made it across.

Well, I was comfortable. Rosco kept looking nervously out the window at how far up the door panel the water level came.

"I don't think this can be good for the car," he said.

I patted Bernadette's dashboard affectionately. "Commodore. Made for Australian conditions," I reassured him. Whether by luck or good design the same procedure worked at another three water crossings on our way out to the Olgas.

Once there we had a good little explore, took several photos, didn't notice any other people, but kept the company of more flies than I've ever seen in one place before or since. At one point the back of Rosco's light blue t-shirt was completely black with the little buggers. Mine was probably as bad, but it made a less impressive picture being a black t-shirt to begin with.

By the time we headed back to where we were staying the water levels had dropped somewhat so Rosco was a bit less twitchy about the crossings.

Still, I'd have to say we were both pretty pleased to be back at the resort and settled in the bar by late afternoon. We were enjoying a cold beer or three and conversing about the day's sights when a bloke in a Park Ranger's uniform came over to our table.

"G'day fellers," he said. "I overheard you talkin' about the Olgas. There'll be no goin' out to see them for a day or two yet, I reckon – the road's closed."

"Good thing we went out today then," I replied innocently.

"No – I mean it's closed *now*. Has been since Friday," he said.

I shrugged. "We were out there today."

"You're game," he responded.

"Or mad," suggested Rosco.

The Ranger looked at me quizzically and asked, "What sort of four wheel drive you got?"

I shrugged again. "I don't. It's a Commodore."

He shook his head and walked away. I heard him mutter, "Bloody tourists…"

*

If you're driving around I reckon you should, whenever possible, take the opportunity to look at things you haven't seen before. Like the song says, "we may never pass this way again". It's particularly true if you're on holiday.

Pete and Rose had lived in Melbourne for a few months before they decided to go on a short vacation to the Coonawarra to spend a few days among the wineries. They went out via an interesting inland route, so as to visit a few other vineyards along the way. So at the end of the holiday, for variety they decided to come back via the Great Ocean Road.

If you've never driven along it you've missed an experience. The views are spectacular. The biggest problem if you're the driver though is that it's frequently hard to watch the scenery. The road winds sharply and often along the coastline, and a moment's distraction could see you over a cliff, into a rock wall, or under an oncoming truck.

Rose was happily being The Tourist in the passenger seat, with lots of "Oohs", "Aahs" and "Look at that's" – which of course Pete could rarely do with any safety.

She insisted on stopping to take photos at frequent intervals until Pete, who was getting understandably weary, said, "No more. I just want to get home. You've got plenty of pictures by now."

Rose wasn't best pleased, but recognizing he was tired, went along with him. A little while later they rounded a bend and the spectacular natural formation called 'London Bridge' came into view.

"Oh! Let's stop and go for a walk out along that! I bet I could get some great photos from there!" Rose exclaimed.

Pete shook his head. "Nope. Sorry. I really do just want to keep going now till we get home. It's been a great trip but I'm stuffed. We'll come back out here sometime soon. London Bridge isn't going anywhere."

Rose lapsed into sullen silence for a while, although by the time they got back to Melbourne her mood had improved.

Sadly that wasn't to last long. It was only a couple of days later that newspapers across the country were carrying front page photos of the spectacular collapse of the sandstone arch under the predictable headline *"London Bridge Has Fallen Down"*.

I don't think poor old Pete has ever been allowed to forget it.

*

The vehicle registration stickers of the last few years have been a big improvement on the old style. Some of the safety messages may have been a bit hokey, though well-intentioned. But for me the great leap forward has been in the adhesive. Nowadays they're fairly easy to apply and, more significantly, easy to remove.

Remember the old type? The only way of taking them off your windscreen was scraping at them with a razor blade. Removing paint was easier!

Steve told me of the time he changed his rego sticker on the morning after a big night out. Laboriously and with much muttering and cursing he scraped off the old green sticker.

That job cost him half an hour and a collection of razor cuts on his fingers. Then he soaked the new blue sticker in warm water and carefully transferred it onto the glass.

Pleased that the job was done, he retired back into the flat for a reviving drink. That evening he was going out again. As he walked past his car he did a double take. There was a green sticker on the windscreen.

He scratched his head, and then the awful truth dawned on him. He looked at his flatmate's car, parked alongside his own in the dual carport.

Yep, sure enough, there was a nice new blue rego sticker stuck amongst several obvious scratches in the glass.

I'll let you imagine the enthusiasm with which he explained this story to the Department of Transport in order to convince them to issue him a replacement sticker.

*

I'd never really seen the point of those 'Baby On Board' signs that became fashionable on cars a few years ago. "So what?" I thought.

I figured it was some sort of request to take more care than usual to avoid running into a vehicle with that sign on it. Given that I had no intention of colliding with anyone if I could help it anyway, that seemed superfluous.

I'm indebted to Julie for explaining to me the true nature of the sign. It's a warning to other drivers.

Depending on the age of the 'baby' on board, the driver could be trying to placate a screaming infant, searching for a tissue or a bottle or a lost toy, attempting to answer a dozen questions about why traffic lights change colour and why they're the colours they are, or any one of a myriad of other distractions.

In short, it's saying: "The person in charge of this vehicle is very probably *not* concentrating on driving. Be very, very wary of them!"

*

There are a few unfamiliar brands of car on the roads of Australia these days. I think many of them are coming from Asia, with some odd Eastern European models thrown in.

I don't have enough first-hand experience to comment on how good or bad any of them are. I'll tell you what *did* catch my eye when riding in one recently.

Printed helpfully on the console of the automatic transmission were the words **"Depress break pedal when shifting out of P or N"**.

Maybe the car is a bit fragile. I know if I'd just bought a brand new car I'd be depressed if the pedal was to break.

*

Multi-level car parks can be a serious drag. They're even worse when there's any sort of construction work happening in or near them.

Jules was visiting a friend in hospital, but first had to find a space in the lofty car park next door. Always a busy place, the hospital parking station chaos was compounded by having building works happening on the top storeys.

After slowly winding her way up the first four levels without success, Jules was confronted with a choice of continuing up either the East or West towers.

With a shrug she took the eastern option and slowly ascended. Progress was repeatedly stalled by cars in front of her stopping to reverse into spaces or make painfully slow and clumsy turns into vacant spots. Then there were the drivers who saw someone walking back to their vehicle. They'd stop and wait for them to get in the car, settle themselves and their passengers, turn on their mobile phone and check their messages and eventually drive out. Only then could the person who'd held up a line of traffic take their place.

After another three storeys of this Jules finally had clear air in front of her – no one else ahead looking for a space. Trouble was, there were no parking spaces left to be had. Suddenly she got to a dead end – the fence behind which the construction work was taking place. Sighing, she negotiated the difficult three point turn required by the barrier.

Then it was back down to the 'junction' floor, avoiding the cars making their own hopeful way up. She kept an eye out for departing cars, but the only space she saw being vacated was filled first by a van coming up, which had been just that bit closer.

The slow climb up the West tower was just as unsuccessful. After a couple of storeys of frustration Jules muttered out loud "This could take all day. I should have packed my lunch!"

As she drove around the next bend, there was a station wagon parked with its tail gate up. There was a blanket spread out on the bitumen behind it, and a couple having a picnic lunch.

If they were at the hospital for the day I guess that had to be easier than driving all the way out to get a good feed then facing another search for a parking spot.

Jules did eventually find a space, not far from the picnickers. Giving them a friendly wave as she passed she wondered (as I did when she related the incident to me) just how appetizing their lunch could have been in the exhaust fume laden air of the car park.

*

If you spend much time on the road, very likely you'll develop considerable familiarity – perhaps more than you'd want – with two particular institutions: roadhouses and public toilets.

I've been in some surprisingly good, and eye-wateringly bad examples of both while traveling in Australia and overseas. With roadhouses I reckon the quality of the place is usually a reflection of the owner/manager. A genial old bastard, a lazy old bastard or a tight-fisted miserable old bastard owner can often be picked by the quality of the food, the temperament of the staff, and the state of the facilities.

It's not uncommon on the bigger highways around Australia to find roadhouses with separate dining rooms and toilets for truck drivers and 'others'. 'Others' may include tourists, commercial travelers, or even locals. I wonder sometimes whose benefit the segregation is for. I think it varies.

In some places I've seen the truckers' diner looking filthy while the 'other' part was reasonably spick and span. My guess is that those owner/managers have no background in the road transport industry themselves, and assume that drivers are grubby, smelly slobs.

Conversely, I've been in roadhouses where the truckers' part of the diner is clean, well-equipped and welcoming whilst the remainder is almost bare except for a couple of near-empty salt shakers, one rat-eared menu, and a thin layer of redistributed grime on the table tops.

Even when the difference isn't quite so extreme, I've on plenty of occasions been left feeling that truck drivers are an elite who should be allowed to enjoy their own and each others company without disturbance. It's bad enough that they have to share the road without sharing precious time off it.

I was impressed by a little stop I found in central southern Queensland. Like a number of such places I've visited, the walls are decorated with photos of drivers and rigs that have passed through there. What caught my eye, though, was the very prominent display of those who'd been killed 'on the road'.

The boss, an ex-driver himself, explained it to me. "Some of these blokes get to thinkin' they're bullet-proof after a while," he said. "Especially them as have never even had a good enough scare to remind 'em that a few tons of metal won't always be enough to protect 'em. Them tons can even get 'em into trouble instead of outta it."

"So I keep this board out here. Partly to remember lost mates, and partly in the hope it'll make 'em think, and drive safe, so we don't lose any more."

I'll drink to that.

*

The more 'free-standing' public toilets (e.g. those in parks or roadside 'comfort stops') on the other hand, while actually the nominal responsibility of some public servant somewhere, are more likely to give a clue as to the type of old bastard who frequents the area.

Touring families tend to get 'nicer' facilities than those you find on routes more commonly used by those who drive for a living. There is, for instance, a better prospect of actually finding toilet paper in a bog on a regular tourist route than in one on something that's more of a 'back road' – that is, assuming you could find a public toilet on such a road. If you're at all fussy, though, it's handy to travel with your own supply of paper!

Some bog papers have clearly been designed by malicious old bastards who anticipate never having to use their own product.

There are the miniscule sheets of what seems to be wax paper. They have the sticking power of Teflon, slide about disconcertingly under your hand, and give the distinct impression of being too slick to be doing their job properly.

Elsewhere on the roster of shame we find the paper that would do service in a belt sander taking the rough spots off knotty pine.

My own least favourite though is the amazingly fragile type that tends to disintegrate even as you try to pull it from the dispenser. If you're not careful you can find yourself clutching a pathetic cluster of paper shreds and ribbons – not hugely useful for the task at hand.

Even if you're really, really delicate enough to get the paper out intact, it's unsettlingly thin. There was an ad long ago where a concerned housewife would hold sheets of different brands of paper up to the light to compare their textures. The stuff I've just encountered in a roadhouse on the outskirts of Sydney is so thin that you don't need to hold it up to the light to see through it.

You can lay a sheet on a page of the phone book and read the names and addresses through it perfectly well. (Yes, I've tried it – I wanted to test my theory.)

What I don't get with this stuff is – *why*? Did some dozy old bastard think "if I make the sheets really really thin, I'll get more in the box, so the box will last longer"? Or was there a thought that it was cheaper to make it this way, so it'd be more 'cost effective'?

Either way, it's false economy. If the paper's so thin you need ten sheets to feel as comfortable (physically, psychologically, whatever) as you would with two at home, then that's what you'll use. The box will empty five times faster, and need replacing five times as often. Or it will run out more often, increasing the odds that someone will kick a hole in the toilet door out of sheer aggravation, meaning increased cost of repairs.

I think more attention should be paid to the hidden costs of bog roll rage.

*

Some years back a small group of us decided to hire a car and spend a week driving around Tasmania. It was meant to be a sort of 'Highway One pub crawl', stopping into at least one pub in every town and village we passed through on the main road around and across the island.

And indeed, we were quite successful in that regard. Each of us took a day's turn as 'designated driver' while the rest sampled the delights of such fine establishments as the Silver Sands in Bicheno, the Regatta Point in Strahan, and the Union in Stanley, to name only a small sample.

We soon found, though, that one of the old bastards in our number had what we called a Japanese bladder – small and yellow. He couldn't just wait between towns and pubs, but was constantly on the lookout for roadside public toilets. "Aah, there's one!" would be his delighted cry, followed by "Pull over please – I won't be a minute…"

*

In these days of environmental awareness and water shortages you see a few compensations and adjustments being made. About the most annoying of them is the 'reduced flush'.

When the button is pressed the cistern releases just enough to 'muddy the waters' so to speak. The contents of the bowl swirl around a bit, but nothing much seems to be accomplished. You either try flushing repeatedly thus defeating the water conservation point of the exercise, or walk away leaving the mess for the next person. You just know they're going to assume you were too lazy or unhygienic to bother flushing after use.

A much better innovation is one I encountered in an excellent restaurant on Queensland's Sunshine Coast. A tap and small basin sit right above the cistern.

When you flush the tap flows for long enough to wash your hands thoroughly, and the waste water flows directly into the cistern ready for the next use.

It's a clever idea, and I'm told it cuts water consumption by 18%. And it encourages people to wash their hands before going back into the restaurant, and I reckon that's also a good thing!

*

Australia's blessed with a lot of good places to stay around the country. The Youth Hostels Australia network is worth a look if you're going traveling.

They've gotten rid of the 'Youth' restrictions a while ago – my former in-laws are YHA members, and while they're young at heart they're also happy to take advantage of the Seniors Card discounts they're offered.

The hostels are mostly clean and well looked after, and you can meet some interesting fellow-travellers from all over the world.

One of my favourite ever nights was in the hostel in the old West Australian gold mining town of Coolgardie. It's almost a ghost town now, but a fascinating place to visit.

This particular night there were eight of us sharing the blokes' dormitory – no two from the same country, and most of us had never met before that afternoon.

It was late and the room was in darkness when there came a scurrying noise from a corner.

"Vas dat a rat?" asked the Swedish backpacker.

"Is not rat, is hamster," replied the Englishman in the bunk below me, in a fine impression of Manuel from Fawlty Towers.

Someone else in the room giggled, so I replied "Don't mind him, he's from Barcelona," in my best John Cleese voice.

A surprisingly plummy, "Basil! What are you up to?" came from the Kiwi on the far side of the room.

"Nothing, Sybil my love," I replied, "Or nothing I'd want you to know about, you old trout."

The giggles were turning into full-blown laughter. For the next half hour or so we lay in the darkness reciting lines from *Fawlty Towers* in eight different accents. I think my favourite moment was hearing Basil's "Don't mention the war!" speech in the unmistakeable accent of the young bloke from Munich.

*

Of course there can be down sides to dormitory accommodation, too. One of the hostels I stayed in out in Central Australia was a basic cinderblock structure with a tin roof. It held about 30-odd blokes.

One night we discovered that three or four of them snored, and snored bloody loudly. It was reverberating off the metal roof and making an unholy row.

After an hour of trying unsuccessfully to sleep with my head stuck under my pillow, I cursed and got up. Grabbing my light calico sheet I headed outside and found a nice piece of bare hillside a hundred metres or so away.

It wasn't hugely comfortable but the sound of the snoring, while audible, was much more tolerable. I fell asleep under the stars quite quickly. When I woke next morning I discovered half a dozen other blokes on the hillside around me, who'd evidently all had the same desperate idea.

The only worse incidence of snoring I can recall was on the old Abel Tasman – the ferry that cruised between Melbourne and Tasmania. There were six of us sharing the cheapest cabin we could get for the overnight crossing.

Two sets of three bunks were set at right angles to each other in a very small room. There was just enough space to open the door and step inside, then clamber into your bunk. The floor, walls and low ceiling were all made of bare metal so the overall effect was like sleeping in a 44 gallon drum.

Two of our number were found to be loud and creative snorers. The resultant din was like having your head stuck in a tin bucket, into which some sadist was loudly pumping "*Songs Of The Humpback Whale*".

It wasn't long before the other four of us retired to the lounge bar for the rest of the night.

*

Talking of difficult nights for sleeping reminds me of a night in a hostel on the Gold Coast. The hostel is now long gone, the old wooden huts now demolished. They were comfortable enough in their day, but pretty basic.

Among the modern conveniences they lacked was air conditioning, or even fans. Another was insect screening.

I was staying there in mid-summer. It was hot and humid. But worst of all as far as I was concerned, it had rained a few days earlier and that had brought out the mosquitoes in plague proportions.

If I tried to cover myself completely in a sleeping bag to keep the little buggers from bleeding me dry, I was overheating and lathered in sweat within a few minutes. As soon as I stuck any part of me out from under cover I'd hear a high pitched whine that was followed by a sharp jab, with itching ensuing soon after.

An hour or so of this was driving me to distraction. I wished it would rain. You don't get mozzies in rain. I pondered that distractedly as I lay there, and remembered why. They can't fly when their wings are wet – something to do with the surface tension or weight of water droplets or something.

Suitably inspired, not to mention desperate, I left my room and headed for the shower block. It was a sufficiently hot night for me not to need to touch the 'H' tap, and even the "cold" water was comfortably lukewarm.

(I'm suddenly reminded of a Scottish old bastard's definition of 'lukewarm' as it applies to a cup of tea: "It lukes warm, but it isnae!")

Meanwhile, back at the old Gold Coast hostel, I smiled as I curled up on the floor under a steadily running shower. For the rest of the night I slept comfortably while mozzies buzzed impotently around the shower stall. It was worth some wrinkled skin to avoid a thousand bites!

*

Any of you who have driven in the scrub anywhere in Australia know that the wildlife can make it a bit of an adventure. And by 'in the scrub' I don't even necessarily mean off the main highway system. I just mean 'out of town'.

I've had run-ins and near-run things with such hazards as kangaroos, emus, cows, even a wedge-tailed eagle. There are other things out there that you don't want to tangle with, either. Old bastard Karl told me of the time he ran over a large black snake on the road outside of Gunnedah. He didn't spot the snake in his rear vision mirror as he drove on. Having heard several stories of angry black snakes wrapping themselves around back axles, he then spent a very nervous time until, and especially *at* the next petrol stop. Fortunately he hadn't picked up an unhappy venomous passenger!

The nastiest wildlife shock I've ever had at the wheel was up in Kakadu. It was about eight or nine at night, dark overcast night, on an unlit stretch of dirt road, and I have to admit I was driving tired. Luckily I wasn't traveling very fast. Coming down a little slope I rounded a bend and said to Helen, "Looks like the fog's forming already."

Then I've suddenly realized that the 'fog' was moving, and slammed on the brakes. What I had thought was a bank of fog was the side of a dirty great water buffalo.

The buffalo stood there looking back and blinking at me a couple of times, then very casually continued its amble off the road back into the bush. By this time Helen had a very firm grip on my leg. "Big buggers, aren't they?" she said quietly.

"Yeah," I agreed, once my heart got going again.

*

Cows aren't as big as buffalos, but the difference doesn't mean much if you collect one at speed. An old bastard I knew in north-east Victoria had a very lucky escape one night. Rew was driving along a back road out behind Tallangatta, from the pub to his parents' place.

It's only a couple of kilometres, and he knows the road like the back of his hand so he was doing a fair turn of speed. All of a sudden as he came round a bend there was a herd of cattle lit up by his headlights. Swerved a couple of them, he reckons, before he took the legs out from under one and it rolled up and over his little Datsun.

Having just missed copping a cow horn through the face, Rew still wore several shards of windscreen and a fierce lump on the head where the roof got lowered on him. Amazingly the car was still drivable, so realizing he was bleeding pretty heavily Rew figured he'd better head for the nearest sizeable town with a medical centre.

The local constabulary there saw the very battered Datsun limp into town and pulled Rew over. Notwithstanding his obvious injuries they got him to blow in the bag.

Well, of course he was over the limit, wasn't he? So he had to leave the car at the side of the road while they took him to the lockup. There at least they called a doctor to come and check him out and clean up his cuts and bruises.

Luckless old bastard Rew was left with a busted car, a few new scars on his mug, and no licence for three months after a judge was "lenient" on him. Mind you, it was nearly worse: the bloke who owned the cattle tried to sue Rew for the loss of some of his supposedly "prize animals".

A couple of us got in Rew's ear about a countersuit for damages because the farmer hadn't shut the gate meant to secure the cows. The whole legal threat quietly went away.

*

There was a team of us working out in central Queensland, basing ourselves in Longreach. Our employer paid for us to hire a few cars in which to travel out to surrounding stations and towns doing some business.

Vinnie and I were on our way out to Barcaldine very early in the trip. Twenty or thirty kilometres out of Longreach an emu started running along beside us.

Emus don't have very big heads, and whatever they keep in those skulls doesn't get used much for thinking, as far as I can see. Around roads especially, they're about the most dangerously stupid critters I've ever encountered. Pheasants in the UK are close contenders in the lack-of-road-sense stakes, but they're a lot smaller in size and can't get up to or maintain the pretty fair turn of speed that an emu's capable of.

The emu that Vinnie and I encountered on this particular day evidently got bored with running alongside us and decided to check out the other side of the car. Without warning it tried to run across in front of us. Vinnie let out a loud curse and swerved – not a good move.

Like a lot of central Queensland roads, this one was made of little more than compressed red earth. The well travelled centre of the road is quite solidly compacted but out by the edges, although it looks the same it's actually pretty much soft powder – better known as bull dust.

As Vinnie swerved he hit bulldust at the side of the road. The left hand wheels sank into the dust and we came to a sudden halt with the car at an uncomfortable 45 degree angle, and some unpleasant damage done to the underside of the chassis.

A passing truck dragged us out of the dust and helped us get the car back to the hire company's office. The bloke in the office nodded sympathetically when we explained what had happened.
"No worries," he said. "I shoulda told you, never worry about hittin' an emu. They're just big bags of shit on skinny legs – don't do much damage. It's alright, I've got one car left. You can have that while I get this one repaired."
"Tomorrow," muttered Vinnie, never the most mild-tempered of bastards. "Right now I need a beer."

So we retired to the Midlander for a few quiet ales, and set off again next morning.

Twenty or thirty kilometres out, in a strangely familiar spot, lo and behold there was another emu – or maybe it was the same one. They all look pretty much alike, except maybe to other emus I suppose. This one ran in front of us almost immediately.

"Not this time, you bastard," growled Vinnie as he gunned the engine. Smacked the big bird with the absolute centre point of the front of the car.

The emu came spinning up over the bonnet and crashed through the windscreen on the driver's side. With a deep sigh Vinnie took his foot off the accelerator and let the car roll to a gentle stop. I was in the passenger seat, with three or four fragments of windshield glass on my lap. Beside me, Vinnie looked like something out of a bad horror movie.

He was covered head to lap in glass fragments, feathers, emu blood, emu innards, and the contents of emu innards. He didn't say a word, and I thought it wisest if I didn't either.

Doing a u-turn at the next convenient spot, Vinnie drove us back into Longreach. As he pulled up outside the rental company headquarters I noticed he was having to struggle to unbuckle his seatbelt, the latch being apparently gummed up with emu anatomy. That gave me the chance to dash inside first to try to soften the blow I knew was coming.

I just managed to get out the words, "We've run into another problem…" when the door flew open behind me. In strides Vinnie, face and shirtfront a mess of glass, gore, feathers and filth. The poor young lass at the reception desk shrieked. The boss came out of his office and stood looking dumbstruck at

Vinnie, who was dripping on the carpet.

Vinnie tossed him the car keys and said, quite calmly, "Any more tips? That last one didn't bloody work."

*

I had an instance a few years back when I was actually quite glad of hitting a kangaroo. We were in my old Commodore on the Newell Highway heading from Brisbane down to Canberra. It was after nine on a starless night and my old mate Rosco was at the wheel.

We were ticking along at 100 kph or so, cruising up a hill about forty kilometres out of Coonabarabran. As we neared the crest of the hill we saw the lights of a semi-trailer obviously coming up the other side of the rise.

Right on the crest a bloody big red kangaroo hopped out of the way of the semi and stopped dead right in front of us. I use the term 'stopped dead' very deliberately, as the roo didn't have a chance. Of course, neither did the front of the Commodore.

The bonnet buckled, and the radiator broke neatly in half. Rosco eased the car to a halt at the side of the road, and we spent an unpleasant few minutes by torchlight scraping bits of shattered marsupial away so we could assess the damage. Luckily it was a cold night and we were able to slowly nurse the car in to Coonabarabran without cooking the engine.

Surveying the damage in the forecourt of the service station, Rosco was quite upset at having broken my car.
"Nothing to apologise for," I reminded him. "If you'd swerved left we'd have hit a tree. Swerve right and we'd have hit the semi. Believe me, you old bastard, Skippy was the best option!"

*

While I'd be happy to travel in the bush with Rosco driving, there are other blokes I know who simply shouldn't be allowed behind a wheel on country roads. Terry was one of them.

Terry was an ardent environmentalist. Now I'm a pretty robust shade of green myself – I've hugged a tree or two in my time and I tended to be rather more sympathetic to his views than many of the crew we worked with. But I don't think I overstepped the bounds of common sense the way he could.

There were four of the boys in the car one night, tootling back from Bundaberg to Bargara with Terry at the wheel. Suddenly he's slowed the car down from 100 kph to about 40 or 50, and switched off the headlights!

Naturally enough there was a bit of an outcry, which I'll politely render down to "What do you think you're doing, you bloody idiot?"

With a very concerned look on his face Terry explained, "Didn't you see the number of insects we've been killing? I think they're attracted by the headlights, so I've turned them off to save the moths."

It apparently took quite a lot of argument, and threats of violence, to convince Terry that the loss of some moths was a better option than wrapping car, driver and passengers around a tree in the darkness.

.o0o.

SOME DIFFICULT OLD BASTARDS

Bert's a genuinely Old old bastard, and a grand bloke. He was telling me about a Senior Citizens' "Wine & Dine" Club he'd joined. Once per month they'd book out a restaurant for a midweek buffet lunch.

The format was that everyone would front up at that month's venue about noon, sit through a speech from the Club President, then at a given signal everyone would amble over to the buffet table and help themselves.

Bert reckoned it was a good chance at a good spread of food and drink at a decent price. The company was a bonus, he said, with most of the other members being good fun to spend an afternoon with.

As with most clubs of any type though, there were a couple of people who in various ways made themselves as popular as a fart in a crowded elevator.

According to Bert the worst offender was a bloke who'd get out of his chair during the President's address, move himself into line with the buffet table, and drop into a 'sprinter's start' crouch.

As soon as the speech was over he'd take off at a run, sometimes getting to the food before the President's bum had even gotten back to the seat. Then he'd proceed to load his plate with the best bits of whatever was on offer: the biggest prawns, the juiciest slabs of meat, the crispest-looking roast spuds.

Everyone else who moved at a more polite, sedate pace was left to pick through his leftovers.

Bert reckoned the problem was that everyone else was too polite to complain or to do anything about it.

"That doesn't sound like you, Bert," I observed.

"Waitin' for me chance," he replied. "One of these days I'll make sure I'm sittin' between him and the tucker."

"You reckon you can outpace him if you've got a bit of a start, eh?"

"Nah. But I can stick me leg out and trip the bugger!"

*

I've had an American postal worker swear to me that this is a true story. I have my doubts, but I also know first-hand how much stranger than fiction the truth can be.

The central figure in this story is an Iraqi living somewhere on the east coast of the US. Presumably he didn't aspire to the glorious afterlife of a suicide bomber, as he decided to make his protesting point by mailing a parcel bomb to one of the government offices in Washington.

At some point in the US postal system someone recognized that the parcel didn't have enough stamps on it for its weight. So it was marked 'Insufficient Postage' and a big Return To Sender sticker was affixed over the top of the Washington address label.

What amazes me here is that the Iraqi had actually written his own real address on the 'sender' part of the mailing label. If he was silly enough to do that, then the final part of the story is truly inevitable.

By the time the parcel was returned to him he'd evidently forgotten what he put in it. He started to open the package, and immediately made the world a little bit safer by taking himself out of it.

*

I was taking a stroll around one of the very posh suburbs of Melbourne. Not that I had, or have, any intention of buying property there (nor much likelihood of affording it either) but I was enjoying some of the gardens and the architecture of some of the older houses.

Suddenly a gate opened in a tall white security fence ahead of me. I can't tell you anything about the house itself as the fence did a fine job of completely hiding the property from anyone on the street.

I couldn't see in, they presumably couldn't see out – even if one of the world's greatest murals was painted on the inside of the fence I'd still reckon it a claustrophobic way to live.

Through the gate came a short, expensively dressed woman. She led on a slim chain a little fluffy white dog. Completely ignoring me she walked the dog a dozen paces or so until they were standing on the footpath outside their next-door neighbours' gate.

She bent down and said something quietly to the dog. It dutifully squatted and laid a fresh mound of crap just by the mailbox.

The woman tugged once on the leash, and then she walked the short return journey home. The dog trotted at her side, evidently happy with its little outing.

I continued my stroll, avoiding the new deposit, and considered what I'd just witnessed.

Had the high fence been erected because the neighbours *really* didn't like each other, and this was another expression of that?

Was this an ongoing feud, with the neighbours likely to respond by scraping the crap up and stuffing it into the offender's letter box?

Or was it living in this self-imposed isolation that led to such a classic display of not caring about others?

Or was she just a bloody ratbag?

*

Jack and Charlie had been hired to fit out a new shop a couple of summers back. The air conditioning hadn't been installed yet, so to catch a bit of breeze they left the front door open while they worked.

Every so often a passer-by would poke their nose in for a stickybeak, and maybe chat for a minute or two.

Charlie was quite glad of this in truth, because Jack was a surly old bastard who was lousy company over the course of a whole day.

They'd just finished putting up the shelving when another visitor stuck his head in the doorway.

"What are you selling?" he asked cheerily, indicating the empty displays.

"Arseholes," growled Jack, annoyed at yet another 'interruption'.

Before Charlie could apologise the visitor smiled and nodded, and said breezily "You're doing well then! You've only got one left!"

Charlie reckons even Jack laughed as the bloke strolled away.

*

This is a tale of revenge, not served cold. Frank had done something to upset Wilko. I'm not sure of exactly what, but whatever it was the unhappiness ran deep.

To make matters worse, Frank was oblivious to the offence he'd caused so made no attempt to put matters right. He was perfectly happy to accept an invitation to come around to Wilko's for pizza after football one Sunday.

Wilko left the game quickly to set his plan in motion while Frank and a couple of mates lingered over a final beer or two. The mates, who were also invited, didn't know the details of the plan but were aware that something was afoot. Intrigued, they made no effort to warn the intended victim.

In due course they all arrived at Wilko's and sat around chatting over drinks while their host flitted in and out of the kitchen and around the flat, obviously preparing the food.

Wilko kept an eye on the level of drinks and when everyone's glasses were empty he announced "Pizza's ready!"

He brought in two steaming fresh home made pizzas and said "I hope you like 'em hot. I'll go get the beers."

"Can't be too hot for me!" scoffed Frank blithely as he grabbed the nearest slice of the pizza that had been put down beside him.

The other guys bit into their slices, and Frank took a huge mouthful of his piece. And immediately changed colour.

All parts of both pizzas looked identical to the casual observer, but the half pie closest to Frank was very different.

For a start, Wilko had spread that section with chilli paste instead of tomato. Then there was a layer of finely chopped habanero hidden under the ground beef, which had itself been liberally laced with cayenne pepper. The 'salami' on Frank's portion was actually extra hot pepperoni. Only the cheese sparsely melted on top wasn't heavy with capsaicin (the stuff that makes chillis hot).

Alternating white, red and purple flushes, Frank grabbed for his beer. Empty!

Despairingly he looked at the others. Their glasses offered no help either. He dived into the kitchen, pushing past Wilko who was leaning beside the doorway.

"What the…?" was Frank's strangled cry as he opened the fridge and found it completely empty of anything liquid. Wilko had been quietly secreting all the drinks into an esky hidden in the garage.

Frank grabbed a glass and rushed to the sink. He turned on the tap – nothing. Wilko had turned off the water at the mains, then quietly gone round and drained every tap in the place.

Scraping the thin layer of frost off the inside of the freezer and stuffing it into his mouth Frank managed to say to Wilko, "Whatever I said, whatever I did – I'm sorry! Okay? I'm really, really sorry!"

With great solemnity Wilko slowly nodded and said, "Apology accepted."

Then he went to the garage and fetched the esky. Frank didn't trust Wilko enough then to accept his advice to drink some milk before a beer. Which is a pity as it was good advice.

The lactose in dairy foods bonds with the capsaicin and neutralizes it, which is why you get yoghurt served with hot curries. All that beer and water do is to distribute the hot stuff a bit more widely around your mouth, throat and insides.

Frank and Wilko remained mates, and once it was explained to him what he'd done to deserve such a diabolical fate Frank swore never to make the same mistake again.

"In that case," promised Wilko, "I promise that in future I will use my chilli powers for good instead of evil."

*

On the Big Island of Hawaii there is an impressive trail called 'Ala Kahakai' – the walk of the people. According to tradition it's the path that was used by the island's inhabitants for many generations to travel along the coastline to attend feasts and ceremonies as well as conducting more mundane business.

The history of the trail is so well established that it's protected by statute. Ala Kahakai must remain open and allow free passage to all.

Unfortunately over the years the precise route of the trail has become unclear. As property values along the coast have soared, land has been bought up. Houses and fences have been built, and Ala Kahakai has become increasingly marginalized. Property rights have been sold to the extent of the high water line in some places. In these spots the 'public trail' is now regarded as the strip between the high and low water lines.

If you're trying to walk the trail at high tide, be prepared to get your feet wet.

Particularly annoying are the wealthy property owners who've chosen to mark the boundary of their place by planting a thicket of spiny mimosa. This lovely plant is covered in sharp thorns at least an inch long. Believe me, you <u>don't</u> want to brush up against it while dodging an incoming wave.

I was walking Ala Kahakai in February, getting increasingly annoyed at a succession of property owners who were forcing me to wade along the trail.

I sat on a rocky point, looking back down at the latest mimosa hedge to have driven me out into the water.

"Bastards reckon they own the beach," I muttered out loud to myself. "I bet they reckon they own the ocean, too."

I'd no sooner said these words when there was a mighty crash off to my right. A whale was breaching. It soared up and thundered back into the water, as close to the shore as I think it was possible for it to be.

It was as if it was answering me, saying, "No, actually <u>I</u> own the ocean here."

Moments later the whale's calf – the next generation of owner – repeated the breaching maneuver. I sat on the rock as speechless as I've ever been in my life.

*

We were having a few quiet beers in the Bookies' Club, with Fred the long-serving manager there.

Conversation got around to discussion of a bloke who might be called a Prominent Identity in the racing industry. The nature of the Club being what it was, Fred was obliged to be a bit diplomatic. But he was well able to make his feelings known.

"I'm not going to call him names," said Fred, "But I don't reckon there's been a marriage in his family for three hundred years."

*

We were in a bar in Broadbeach watching a good blues band. Rather I should say we were *trying* to watch the band.

It was a small bar, an excellent three piece band, and a big crowd.

The biggest problem for us wasn't really the size of the crowd. It was the size of the bloke standing between us and the stage. The crush was too great for us to move to a better position, so although we could hear the music quite well all that we could see was the broad expanse of the guy in front of us.

And when I say broad expanse, I mean broad expanse. It wasn't just that he was tall – over 180 centimetres if not by much, but he was two men wide. Maybe only a bloke-and-a-half across the shoulders, but by the time you got below the line of his armpits he seemed to expand out like a weather balloon.

He was perched on two bar stools, one under each butt cheek, and created the same effect for those behind him as having a billboard erected across a scenic view.

Quite suddenly, right in the middle of a song in fact, the big man got up and lumbered out of the bar. The effect was like a bowling ball rolling through ankle-high grass. People were simply squeezed out of the way. I hope none were actually squashed under his passage.

At last we could see the band!

"Mohammed must be in the building," quipped Ross. "The mountain's moved!"

*

I really do try not to listen in to other people's conversations but sometimes you can't help but catch something that draws you in. It's a bit like the morbid fascination of staring at a road accident.

One such conversation that captured my attention was in the foyer of a tourist resort. I was waiting to talk to someone faintly helpful at the Reception desk when I chanced to hear an animated conversation between a young couple waiting for a porter.

Actually 'conversation' is the wrong word. It was one way traffic with the poor girl unable to get a word in edgeways.

"Always order big!" the bloke directed her. "Get the biggest you can get of everything. Biggest serve you can fit on your plate at the breakfast buffet. Biggest beer you can get on the bar tab. The biggest hotel room you can get for the price. Whatever – always go for the biggest of everything. Biggest is best."

What fascinated me was that the individual expounding this philosophy wasn't much over a metre and a half tall. I wonder how seriously the girl took the "Biggest is best" line coming from a bloke whose eyebrows lined up with her nipples.

*

One of the girls I've worked with over the years was a South American named Mari. She was quite pretty, but could be a little odd. I guess some of it could be chalked up to 'cultural differences', but she had times of being infuriating.

Soon after she joined the group I was working for, I was hosting a dinner party for several of the gang. I thought it would be nice to invite her so that she could get to know a few of us outside the work environment.

She was keen on the idea, so I asked all the usual pre-dinner party questions: any allergies? Any foods you don't eat? You're not vegetarian or Jewish?

"No, no," she replied. "I'll eat anything!"

Secure in her emphatic reply, and already knowing the tastes of my other guests I set about planning the five-course menu.

The following Saturday night the party got under way. With seven guests sitting around the table chatting and drinking I brought out the appetizer.

"What's this?" asked Mari.

"Home-made cognac pate," I replied.

"What's that?" she asked.

"A sort of paste made from chicken livers and cognac," explained Jenny, who was one of the other guests.

'Uh-oh, here it comes,' I thought, expecting a negative reaction to the chicken livers.

Instead she said "Oh! Cognac! That's brandy, isn't it? I don't like brandy." She contented herself with eating the dry crackers I'd served as accompaniment.

A little later I brought out the soup. "That smells good," enthused Jan.

"House specialty," I replied, "Cream of white onion with nutmeg."

Mari's spoon stopped halfway to her mouth. "Onion? Oh – I don't like onion."

So she grazed on the oatcakes I'd laid out to go with the soup.

Next up was the entrée – individual cheese soufflés. You guessed it – "Oh, I don't like cheese…" This time there wasn't even a side dish for her to nibble on.

We got to the main course. Well, seven out of eight of us did. Mari looked into the serving dish full of carefully prepared beef stroganoff and said "Oh, mushrooms! I don't like mushrooms."

With a collective sigh the rest of us left her most of the herbed baby potatoes and honey-glazed carrots.

It was only dessert that she attacked without qualm. Evidently there was nothing to object to in a chocolate pavlova!

One of the other guests drove Mari home and told me later that she'd asked to stop at a roadside hot dog stand because she was 'still a little hungry'.

I wonder whether the words "I'll eat anything!" actually have a completely different meaning in Venezuelan.

*

A while later some friends threw a costume party with a 'circus' theme. Mari came dressed as a cowgirl. That seemed a bit tenuous, but since the host was wearing a giant chicken suit there was little point in arguing.

Part of Mari's costume was a twin holster complete with two shiny six-guns.

At one point Rosco, clowning around appropriately for his Bozo outfit, decided to re-enact one of his favourite scenes from the movie "Blazing Saddles".

Having neither the height nor the skin colour of Cleavon Little, he had to content himself with putting one arm round his own throat, holding a gun to his head with the other hand, and shouting "Nobody move or the short guy gets it!"

A few of us played along and delivered the appropriate lines of dialogue in response. We all laughed and Rosco gave the gun back to Mari.

Some time and several drinks later, one of the blokes at the party said or did something to annoy Mari.

"You stupid man! I shoot you!" she shouted and fired one of her pistols at him from quite close range. To most onlookers' astonishment a large black powder burn appeared on the white shirt of the offender's costume.

Rosco went as white as the shirt. "The bloody things are loaded!" he exclaimed.

"Is just blanks," dismissed Mari.

"I had that at my head! I could have killed myself!"

"No," she shrugged, "I not give you the gun with the real bullets."

I must remember never to go to a costume party in Venezuela. If carrying a loaded gun to a gathering of friends is considered normal or necessary I think I'd rather avoid the social life there.

*

The dishonest bastards. They're out there. You know they're out there. Some of them operate outside the law. Some of them operate in ways that are, strictly speaking, legal, but any reasonable bastard knows what they're doing just isn't right.

I remember seeing a TV interview some years back with a very senior minister in the State Government of the time. He gave the interviewer a broad smug grin and said something to the effect of: "You might reckon I'm a crook. I might nod and say 'maybe you're right' – but ya can't bloody prove it, so I don't care!".

Eventually of course it was proved, but way too late to do anything about it. By the time the evidence came to light the bloke was beyond the reach of any court. Any in this world, anyway.

*

Sammy's a courier who spends his working hours delivering parcels to people's doors. He told me this story first, which I then heard again from one of the other people involved, so I'm pretty confident it's the true story of one of the dead-set stupidest crooks in the country.

Sammy knocked on the door of this place. A very dark skinned Asian-looking bloke answered the door. Now that didn't bother Sammy, since that description wouldn't go far astray on him either. But he did raise an eyebrow because the name on the parcel was something like Mrs. Gloria Macnamara.

"Got a package for Mrs. Macnamara," says Sammy.

"Ah – she's not here," says the bloke. After a quick pause he says, "I'll take it – I am a friend of hers."

Well, it wasn't one of those highly secure deliveries where you have to see the ID of the person it's addressed to, so Sammy shrugs and says, "Righto. Just sign here to say I've delivered the parcel."

So the bloke dutifully signs the form and Sammy goes on his way.

A day or so later Sammy gets called into the office. There's a copper in there, standing beside the boss. It turns out that Mrs. Macnamara's place was robbed on the day of the delivery. Amongst the stuff nicked were the items in the package. The police knew that because the empty box was found near the front door.

Sammy pulled out his docket book and checked it. "There's the signature of the bloke who signed for it," he said, and handed the book over while describing what he could remember of the guy's appearance.

The bloke had signed in very clear handwriting. The copper started to make a note of the name, saying, "Not much point of course – bound to be a phony..."

Nope. It wasn't. The copper recognised it as belonging to someone who only lived a couple of houses away from Mrs. Macnamara, and who'd been interviewed already as part of the routine check of the neighbours.

A burglar who signed his own name. Not a clever bastard.

*

Macca runs bus tours – good ones – for social clubs in south-east Queensland. He's a well-organised Old Bastard and his tours run as close to clockwork as possible (tricky when you're herding 42 keen drinkers around half a dozen wineries!).

He had a tour organised around one of the wine districts a few hours out of Brisbane, but when the weekend came the weather turned vile. So foul that flash floods cut off the town that was intended to be the overnight 'base' of the tour.

Not having much choice, Macca turned the bus around and took everyone home. He then rang the various businesses that were to have been visited to let them know what he'd done, and to check they were okay in the rising waters.

The various wineries and restaurants that had been booked for tastings and meal stops were all fine. They were happy to refund Macca's deposit, or credit it to a rescheduled tour. They appreciated the call, and understood it was nobody's fault.

The exception was the motel which had been booked for the night, and which had demanded a very hefty deposit to cover the thirty or forty expected guests. Macca regretfully explained that as the police had advised that the town was cut off by floodwaters he wouldn't be bringing his busload in that night.

"Minimum 24 hours notice of cancellation or no refunds," responded the motel owner.

Macca patiently explained that it was a flash flood. The road had only been cut that day – the intention had been to brave the weather but that just didn't turn out to be possible.

"Minimum 24 hours notice of cancellation or no refunds," responded the motel owner.
Our bus driving mate did his best to be reasonable and patient. Could the deposit be held for the next tour – he'd taken several busloads there before, after all?

"Minimum 24 hours notice of cancellation or no refunds," responded the motel owner.

So that was the end of that. The motel kept the money. And if there were people in town flooded out and looking for a bed for the night I'd be willing to bet the motel wasn't letting those rooms go for free.

And Macca will definitely NOT be including that motel on any future trip.

The only reason I'm not mentioning the name of the motel is that I'm sincerely hoping that the lousy bastard owner goes broke sooner than later, and I don't want the new proprietors to be tarred with the sin of the current one.

.oOo.

THE BASTARD'S NOT WELL

If you've never had to suffer from kidney stones, consider yourself bloody lucky.

I'm told by experienced mothers that the pain is the only thing they've known that's worse than child birth. I haven't had a baby so I won't comment on the comparison, but I do know that they're horrible damn things.

Kidney stones, I mean. Not babies. Usually.

Anyway, you may not know that the medical term for kidney stones is renal calculus.

That makes sense to me. My recollection of calculus when I was doing maths at high school is that it was hard and a pain in the lower parts of the anatomy.

*

I don't normally regard death as a funny thing. But I have to admit, across the globe, and across history, humankind has come up with some odd rituals and traditions around how we treat the departed.

Well, odd to the people who are 'outside' that belief system or tradition. Those on the 'inside' doubtless don't see a problem.

Back in the 1800's there was a bit of a stir in the Australian press when a prominent Hindu bloke's wife died. The lady in question was cremated, which didn't raise an eyebrow.

The shocked reaction came when the bereaved husband took some of her ashes, stirred them into a goblet of wine, and drank her!

And some of us complain about a bit of cork taint in our shiraz!

*

One of the more ancient traditions is that of being buried with favourite animals. Maybe for food, maybe for company, maybe for some religious symbolism – the Egyptians did it, the Vikings did it, I think lots of cultures have done it.

I thought the idea had died out (excuse the expression) in the modern, Western world.

Not quite, it seems. Looking at one of the ancient tombs up in the Orkneys, an Aussie in the tour group piped up and mentioned, quite casually, that 'back home' he had a freezer full of the frozen corpses of all the budgies he'd kept as pets. It was written into his Will, he explained, that the birds should be buried with him when he died.

The group went very quiet, and the conversation was awkwardly moved into other paths.

The tour guide who related this story to me explained that everyone else in the party immediately realized why this bloke was single.

It could have been worse. His favourite pets could have been Irish Wolfhounds.

*

I really do wonder about some parents, and the names they give their kids.

There are the ones who fancy something exotic and 'foreign'. Gaelic names are high on this list, which is fine for families where that's the bloodline. Trouble is, not many people speak the Gaelic any more so the link between how a word looks and how it sounds can be a problem.

Maybe that's why we get Ruraidh spelt as Rory, and Siobhan as Shivaun. Tough on the small Muraidh trying to learn how to spell her name when it doesn't look like the letter/sound combinations she's learning at school or on the TV.

Then there are the aspirational names. There was a professional footballer in the US a little while back who'd been christened 'Lawyer'. I'm not sure if they'd have been disappointed in his career choice, but given the money NFL players can make, perhaps not!

The parents who actually christened their little girl 'Princess' – well, they're just asking for trouble, aren't they?

And then there are the weird spelling variations.

Sometimes I think it comes from liking the sound of a name but not knowing how to spell it. The Gaelic names come into that category. So too, I suspect is another US variant I've seen – Duhwayan. I believe it's pronounced "Dwayne".

Other times it's just sheer pretentiousness – being 'different' for the sake of it. The letter K seems strangely popular for this. Krystal. Mikhael for anyone who's not Russian. Kraigg.

Being defiantly independent is one thing, but the poor bastard kid will spend years sighing and explaining to clerks, office staff and people on the phone, "No, it's Craig with a K. And two Gs on the end. Sorry – blame my parents."

*

I was in Lismore Hospital a summer or two ago. I was sharing a ward with big Pete, both of us in there with ticker trouble. We've wound up becoming good mates I'm glad to say, but for the first few days we each wondered if the other was some sort of jinx.

First, the shower in our room broke. The whole hose fitting snapped clean off the wall. Now, I'll admit that it was in my hand when it came apart, but the only thing I'd done was turn the tap on. I reckon whoever was in the shower before me had done the damage.

Then it was the angiogram machine itself. We'd both been prepped and readied to have the needle and the very long tube inserted.

Pete was in first and was actually on the table, waiting for the anaesthetist to do his thing. Then came one of the words you least want to hear in an operating room: "Oops!"
There was a problem with the machine that was on the end of the tube. A blown fuse, a burned out wire, or a fault in the bit that goes 'ping' – who knows? Whatever the problem was, it meant there'd be no more angiograms that day. Not for Pete and not for me.

It took a couple of days for the machine to be fixed. But Lismore is a regional hospital. The medical specialists are shared around between a few places. So it happened that once the angiogram machine was working again, there was nobody to work it for another couple of days.

We'd been expecting to go home after only a day or two in hospital, so Pete and I were starting to feel a little 'cabin-crazy'. News that both the machine and the team to operate it would be together at the same time cheered us both up considerably. We looked out the window – the sun was shining, the sky was clear, and the world was good.

The sun was shining. Boy, was it shining. Once again Pete and I were prepped and ready. This time I was going to go first. We lay in our ward, chatting about how we were looking forward to getting home.

A very embarrassed-looking nurse walked in. The same one who'd shaved our groins (again) ready to have the needle stuck in. She hadn't looked embarrassed then. I suppose that was part of the job that happened all the time. Being the bearer of bad tidings probably happened a lot too, but these weren't the usual bad tidings.

"Sorry guys," she said. "The air-conditioning in the theatre room has broken down. It's forty-eight degrees and rising in there. I'm afraid the doctors aren't prepared to work in those conditions. They – ah – don't think it would be good for you, either."

Reluctantly we agreed, not that we had any say in the matter, of course.

The story has a happy ending, thankfully. The air-con was repaired later that afternoon, and the medical team were scheduled to be in Lismore the next day. The angiogram machine didn't break down – it went 'ping' and everything. The stuff shaved off our groins didn't inconveniently grow back overnight.

Pete and I both had our angio procedures. Both went well, and we both, finally, got to go to our respective homes. And when we got home we both immediately complained about the lack of air-conditioning (the temperature was still over forty) and found ourselves pining for our ward.

.o0o.

THE OLD BASTARD AT WORK II

On and off over the years I've done a few stints in different bits of the Public Service. I've even had a few bosses tell me I was good at some aspects of it. Mind you, I've had others tell me quite the opposite. But I'm not really suited for it.

I especially can't take the jargon seriously. Every department has its own, and there's some that crops up right across the bureaucracy. It's probably there in private enterprise, too. It's like a code that protects the secrets of the agency, or department, or company.

Jargon is insidious. If you're not careful it creeps inside your head. One of the key indicators for me that I should get out of the Public Service was the fact that I was using phrases like 'key indicators' in normal conversation.

When I was young I got accused by some of the local kids of using "too many big words". In hindsight, I figure it was because I loved to read whereas they didn't, or couldn't.

Some people do get a bit pretentious with their vocabulary (hmm – was that an example?). One of the best I heard was a judge complaining about a prosecutor's overblown language, accusing him of "gratuitous philological exhibitionism". Now that's the pot calling the kettle black.

That judge would have shaken his head at a manager I knew who was prone to never use one syllable when three could be called upon. Telling one of her staff that he didn't know what he was talking about, she couldn't even let it go at, "You are not in full possession of the facts, Wayne."

She had to add, "You have an unevolved perspective."

*

Being a good or bad boss has nothing to do with gender. I've known excellent supervisors both male and female and some absolute shockers likewise. But for whatever reason a mean-spirited woman in a position of authority seems to generate a greater depth of bad feeling.

Freda was a classic example. She would spend her day watching everyone on her team like a hawk, thus actually making herself the least productive person in the room. If somebody left their desk she'd note it on a pad on her desk, and time how long they were away.

One morning she marched up to Glen just after he'd sat back down after a little while away. In a voice that was intended to be heard by everyone in the vicinity she said, "You've been gone for over fifteen minutes. Where were you?"

"In the men's room," was Glen's calm and quiet reply.

Freda looked down her nose at him, and upped the volume of her voice even further. "I think that fifteen minutes is far too long to be in the toilet. What were you doing in there?"

Glen looked up at her eye to eye and matching her decibel for decibel replied, "Not that it's any of your business, but working for you's given me piles, and it takes me a while to shove 'em back in!"

To make matters worse for Freda, word got around (courtesy of some of the nightclub goers in the office) that after a few drinks she became rather sexually aggressive. Predatory, even.

One day she was berating Joe for not working quickly enough. "You couldn't work in an iron lung!" she shouted at him.

Unfazed, Joe shrugged. He didn't need to shout, he had a voice that carried without much effort. He just looked at Freda thoughtfully and replied, "A job working on your back? You'd be a natural."

*

At one point I worked in an office with a bloke known to all and sundry as Bozo. His grasp of reality and his place in it often seemed uncertain.

He had a number of quirks, like a propensity for driving four hours each way to watch a drive-in movie (on his own) even if the same film was showing at a cinema in town.

As you might guess from that sort of driving for its own sake, Bozo was a big car fan. At one point he was rebuilding the engine of an old Holden at home. He related this story of his mother berating him one afternoon, demanding that he get the bits and pieces of dismantled motor off the floor of the dining room before friends arrived for a dinner party that evening. He was left to address the situation while Mum got on with preparing the dinner.

Eventually she emerged from the kitchen, ready to lay out some cold appetisers on the table just before the guests arrived. As Bozo described it, she let out a terrible shriek and began to loudly and very unfairly abuse him. He'd done what was asked – he'd picked the engine parts up off the floor. Nobody had actually told him *not* to move them up onto the dining table, which was the nearest available flat surface. It hadn't been malicious or mischievous, it just didn't occur to him that it wasn't a good idea, even when he noticed the oil stains he was leaving on the white linen tablecloth.

Within the office, Bozo's eccentricity reached its highest expression when he was on the phone. I hate to imagine what the poor buggers on the other end of the line must have felt like, but just hearing Bozo's side of a conversation was often enough to crack up the whole office.

One afternoon we couldn't help but hear him:
"Hello, can I help you? What? Oh – I rang *you*? Did I? Um – do you have any idea why? Pardon? Oh – who *am* I?"
Bozo then hung up on the poor confused soul.

Another time he was on the phone to an accountant who clearly had a lot on his mind. We could hear the crackling drone of the voice coming down the line for long spells at a time, punctuated occasionally by Bozo's "uh-huh", "yes" and "I see".

Eventually the bloke must have stopped for breath, because Bozo was at last able to get a word in.
"Look," he said, "I don't really know what you're talking about. But then again, I don't really know what *I'm* talking about either so I guess that doesn't matter. Go on."

There was a brief silence, then the accountant started up again. I guess they deserved each other.

*

It was the relatively early days of what is now called Information Technology. The Internet was just starting to catch on in offices across Australia and not everyone had quite grasped it yet.

Barney had just written a pretty scathing letter to a client who'd annoyed him, and in the heat of the moment sent it off as an e-mail.

Almost immediately his temper cooled and he realized that his intemperate e-mail was only going to make matters worse.

"I can't delete it after I've pressed 'Send', can I?" he asked optimistically.

"Well, you can, but it's already in the system so it won't really help," he was told.

Barney pondered for another moment. "It's alright!" he said suddenly, "I'll stop the e-mail!" and promptly pulled the phone plug out of the wall.

A few years before that there was a 'Help Line' set up for users of a new software package which the federal government had released. A call came in one afternoon from an accountant who'd been in business for decades, but had only just acquired his first computer.

"This disc you've sent me doesn't work with my machine," he complained.

The puzzled Help Line worker asked him to explain exactly what he'd done when he tried to install the software. He went through the process step by step having it confirmed with a, "Yes, that's right, go on."

Finally the irritated accountant was told, "Well, that all sounds okay. Your system should be fully set up and ready to go."

"But it isn't right," he persisted.

"What's on your screen?"

"Press any key to continue. That's the problem. My machine doesn't have an 'Any' key."

This story has become urban legend, I think, but I swear it's true. It was me that took the call.

*

Working in the more rarefied atmosphere of bureaucracy, while enormously satisfying and rewarding for some people, is also not for everyone.

One of the absolutely nicest blokes I've met in the US is a genial old bastard named Bill. He spent quite a few years in Washington D.C. as a professional lobbyist. I gather he was pretty good at it, too.

Now though, he's concierge at a very nice resort hotel. He spends his day helping people organize their holiday so that they get the most fun and best value out of their time.

"My old job was interesting," he told me. "And it did introduce me to my wife, so I have that to be thankful for. But this..." he said, patting a rack of colourful brochures. "Every day I go home *knowing* I've made someone's life a little happier. A real person – someone I've met face to face, known their name and shaken their hand. *That's* job satisfaction."

The so-called 'service industry', right across the planet, needs more people like Bill.

*

Enquiry counters and service counters can be hugely frustrating places, whichever side of them you're on, and often for the same reason. There are few things worse than not being able to help someone, or be helped, because 'the rules' won't allow it.

Now, I've long regarded the rulebook as the last resort of the unimaginative, and there's not much that annoys me more than being told that "there's no reason for this decision, sir – it's just our policy." It's an excuse for people who can't be bothered thinking of a solution to someone else's problem.

One of the best stories I've heard about this kind of dozy bastard came from Sid - a bloke I know who was trying to get his stepson's name changed by deed poll. Amongst the two dozen or so bureaucratic hoops he had to jump through was providing at least three photos of the boy for identification purposes.

Sid duly arrived at the counter with what he thought were three decent ID photos: the Grade 1 school photo, a passport photo taken at about the same time, and the Grade 2 school photo.

The bloke behind the counter looked at the snaps, and then handed them back to Sid saying, "I can't accept these".

"Why not?" asks Sid, puzzled.

"He looks older in this one," says the genius, tapping the Grade 2 photo.

*

In a similar vein of bureaucratic absurdity: a bloke I know (let's call him Clive) fronted up at the Customer Service desk of an institution that had better remain nameless. He was there to open an account of some sort.

The person behind the counter explained that two forms of identification would be required.

Clive scratched his head. "I'm not sure what I've got on me… Hang on, I'll look for two that match," he said, only half-jokingly. Clive smiled.

The Service person didn't react for a moment, and then said tonelessly, "One of them has to have your address on it."

With a worried look on his face, Clive pulled an official-looking piece of paper from his bag.

"Um… this is all I've got on me. It's a summons to appear on a fraud charge…"

"Is the address correct?"

"Well, yes…"

"That'll do."

Presumably the Customer Service person either didn't listen, didn't comprehend, or didn't care because it wasn't their money at risk. I am SO pleased I don't do business with this particular institution.

*

Of course, you also get those on the other side of the counter who'll try to twist the rules to suit themselves. I spent a little while working for the old Commonwealth Employment Service (now part of Centrelink) in a fairly small country town.

There was a young bloke there who was quite keen to stay on the dole, but he knew the rules said he had to attend a certain number of job interviews in order to do so. What's more, he had to present an 'acceptable standard of appearance' at such interviews. His trick was to take his pet rat to the interviews with him at jobsites or in the CES, and bring it out of his pocket to put off whoever he was talking to. The girls in our office particularly hated it whenever he came in.

One day I called him in to see me before I sent him to an interview with a mechanic who I knew wanted an offsider. The kid arrived on time, and within two minutes had his rat out and playing on the table in front of me.

I put my hand out, the rat ran up my arm and promptly hunkered down on my shoulder.
"Right," I said. "Your little mate is obviously happy here. I'll keep an eye on him for you till you get back from the interview."

"Hey! You can't do that! Giz me rat back!" he whined.

"When you get back from the interview," I repeated.

"But he's me pet! You dunno how to look after him…"

"I reckon he's safe for an hour or two," I replied. "I looked after rats and mice in the zoo for a while." (I didn't have the heart to tell him I was raising them to feed to the snakes.)

The kid slouched out with his face tripping him and went off to his interview.

I rang my mate the mechanic in the time between the interview and when the kid got back, and got a glowing report of how good he'd been. I warned him that if he gave the kid the job he could expect to have him arrive together with his rat on the first day.

"No worries," the mechanic replied. "I've got a cat here who'll appreciate it."

*

Ron's an old bastard who works as the maintenance man in a nursing home. It's a pretty new establishment so he doesn't have a lot of big jobs to do.

There's enough to keep him busy, though, especially with some residents who have their 'funny little ways'.

Some of them, I think, just enjoy the company of someone who's not on the nursing staff. So they'll get him in to tighten up door handles in their room, or check a perfectly good tap washer or power point. It's an excuse for a chat more than anything else. And when he's not busy Ron doesn't mind.

He told me about Mrs. Brown, an old dear who complained that she was having trouble with the smoke alarm in her room. Every so often it would activate itself, beep a couple of times, then stop again.

"There must be smoke getting into it from somewhere," she grumbled, "I don't wants to be burned in me bed."

Ron took the cover off the unit and found that everything looked okay.

The next time Mrs. Brown complained about it, a few days later, he replaced the battery even though the one already in the unit was itself still quite new.

A few days later her room number turned up on Ron's jobs sheet yet again, with another complaint about the smoke alarm. This time though it was corroborated by a nurse who'd been in the room at the time the alarm seemingly switched itself on and off.

Having repeatedly checked the alarm unit itself Ron figured it was time to do some detective work, especially as Mrs. Brown maintained her conviction that there had to be smoke coming from somewhere.

Having a nurse back up the story ruled out the remote possibility that Mrs. Brown had been sneaking an occasional cigarette in her room.

Perhaps the room was somehow getting traces of smoke blow in from the kitchen? No – the smoke detectors in the kitchen itself weren't going off, so that seemed unlikely.

A thorough search outside in the grounds anywhere near Mrs. Brown's room failed to turn up any possible sources of smoke.

And still the alarm kept being reported as going on and off at odd hours.

With the only apparent explanation left being some sort of haunting, Ron decided he'd just have to remove and replace the whole unit. Maybe it was the sole defective one in the entire bunch that the home had been fitted out with.

So he brought a ladder into Mrs. Brown's room, climbed up, and removed the entire smoke detector and alarm apparatus.

As he pulled it away from the ceiling he exclaimed, "A-ha! Mrs. Brown, I've found your problem!"

There was an ants' nest in the roof space. Evidently ants would occasionally wander down into the unit and disturb either the sensor or alarm mechanism.

Stubbornly oblivious to Ron's attempts to explain, even while he worked to remove the offending nest, Mrs. Brown insisted, "I know what the problem is! There's smoke getting in from somewheres!"

"Yes," said Ron with a sigh. "Smoke with legs."

*

The nursing home staff discovered another unexpected and unusual problem when they first moved into their flash new premises.

Nearby is a large concrete water tower. These are usually rather unattractive structures, but the local council had made an effort to make this one interesting.

It's been garlanded with coloured light bulbs that shine out at night against the towers concrete walls that are floodlit in a bright blue glow. It looks a bit like a giant psychedelic martini glass.

Unfortunately for the nursing home staff, the tower is very visible from a number of the rooms in the dementia wing.

Until new, thicker opaque curtains were hung in the affected rooms there were nightly panics by some of the residents who could clearly see a UFO hovering right outside!

*

It's a sad thing that for some families the nursing home gets used as a dumping ground for relatives who nobody can be bothered with any more. I appreciate that sometimes things can reach a point where it's neither practical nor reasonable to look after a frail or infirm elderly person at home. I understand that first hand. What bothers me though is that sometimes the poor souls seem to be forgotten once they're deposited in The Home.

I'm one of a small number of regular visitors there. I'm used to seeing the same few faces, and don't normally have trouble finding a space in the car park. The exceptions of course are Mothers Day and Christmas Day, when consciences are evidently jogged and appearances put in.

Colleen is a dear friend of mine who works in an Old Peoples' Care Centre. It was all I could do to cope with some of the things I used to see and hear when visiting my Mum in her (quite excellent) Home. I've no idea how staff deal with it day in and day out.

Colleen told me about one laconic lady in her eighties who remarked in passing that when she died she wanted her ashes scattered in the local shopping mall. When asked why she wanted such an unusual 'resting place' she explained, "I know at least then my daughters will visit me a couple of times a week."

*

One occupation I've had quite a bit of trouble with over the years is bouncers, or 'hotel security'. I suppose there must be some reasonable ones out there but from my experience it's like career politicians: most people who really really want the job shouldn't be allowed to hold it.

The casual violence I've seen some of them use is more than bad enough, but what really ticks me off is the sheer mule headedness I keep running into. Some of the 'reasons' for refusing admission that I've heard have been downright bizarre.

I was stopped at the door of one pub because I was "wearing gang colours".

Puzzled by this I checked the plain white polo shirt I was wearing. "Am I missing something?" I asked, trying to be reasonable.

"Yer hat," the ox indicated.

Oh. Right. A multi-coloured flat cloth cap with a Guinness logo on it. The pub must have been having trouble with marauding gangs of Irish golfers.

*

Another time I was 'refused entry' because I was walking with the aid of a cane.

"Can't come in with that," grunted one of the two white-shirted lumps at the door.

"It's a walking stick," I explained as patiently as I could. "I've got a crook knee."

"Can't come in with that."

"Look, do you want me to bring you a medical certificate or a disabled sticker or something?"

"Don't care. Can't come in with that. Looks like a weapon to me."

It's probably as well that one of the old bastards I was with led me away, before I lost my temper and investigated how good a weapon my cane might be.

*

One of the most frustrating things is that different standards seem to apply depending on if you're male or female. I've seen quite reasonable blokes 'barred' because they were "too drunk" to be let in, while a gaggle of girls so hammered they'd lost the use of consonants were allowed to stumble and stagger in.

The fact that one or more of the girls looked likely to fall out of her dress at any moment may have been in their favour.

Gill and I were in town together one night. We were dressed exactly the same, in jeans and collared t-shirts from a sports club we both belonged to. Feeling like a quiet drink we wandered over to one of Brisbane's older hotels.

Gill walked in and headed for the beer garden. As I went to follow her a heavy hand landed on my shoulder.

"Can't come in. Dress regulations," was the grunt.

"What?" I exclaimed.

"No sports clothes," he said, jabbing a meaty finger into the logo on my shirt.

Noticing my absence, Gill came back to find out what was going on. I pointed her out to the bouncer and said, "Look, she's wearing exactly the same thing, and you let her in."

With barely a glance he replied, "Yeah. She looks different in it than you."

I looked at the very different ways our curves filled our shirts and couldn't honestly argue with him.

*

The Valley is a nightclub area in Brisbane, for those of you who don't know of it. It has a collection of bouncers of various sizes and temperaments, some of whom I've actually gotten on okay with.

One young bloke I encountered was clearly a fairly simple soul, good with simple orders. His simple order had obviously been, "Ask for ID and check the age of everyone that comes into the bar". And so he did.

It was the first time I'd been asked for 'proof of age' for over twenty years, but he was very polite about it so I took it with a grin. The same went for the blokes I was out drinking with, and a couple of them were well on the far side of fifty.

As we sat at the bar we noticed a little old lady a few seats along. She'd sip away at her port and lemonade, and then when it was finished she'd get up and leave. A few minutes later she'd come back inside, resume her position and order another drink.

When that was done she'd do the same thing again. I wasn't sure if this was a kind of dottiness, a long-established cigarette ritual, or something cannier. After a couple more repetitions of the cycle I approached her.

"Excuse me – I couldn't help noticing you keep leaving the bar after each drink. Is everything alright?" I asked.

She beamed back at me and said "Fine, but thank you for asking. You see, every time I come back inside that nice young man at the door wants me to prove I'm old enough to drink here. I'm 83 and it's lovely to have a fella keep asking me if I'm over 17."

*

Wildlife photography can be a teeth-grindingly frustrating hobby.

I sat on a little rocky outcrop at Waikoloa (Hawaii), patiently watching a green turtle as it very gradually made its way towards the shore.

After 45 minutes or so it reached a point where I could get a decent shot when it surfaced to breath (which they don't do often).

Right then I heard a voice behind me cry, "Ooh look! A turtle!"

The blonde woman who I'd heard dashed past me, dragging her diving mask and snorkel into place as she ran into the water. Of course, she lunged as close to the turtle as she could so she could get a good look at it. Of course the turtle immediately turned tail and headed back out to sea.

I was left with a photo of the top of the blonde's snorkel tube and her ample behind breaking the surface of the water as she swam off after the object of our mutual attention.

*

Modelling is perhaps an even more transitory occupation than acting. A good actor who can play character roles could have a career for life. If all they have is a "look" it's not likely to last anything like as long. That's even more true for a model.

Allison is a friend of mine who has made a successful living in front of cameras for more years than she'd appreciate my mentioning. She explained to me that the stages of a really first class model's career can be characterized by imagining the comments of a big producer or advertising executive.

Struggle. "Who's Allison Jones?"

Success. "Get me Allison Jones."

Success and a high rate of pay. "Get me an Allison Jones type."

Time passes. "Get me a young Allison Jones."

More time passes. "Who's Allison Jones?"

*

Cab driving is a job I confess that I don't fancy. The hours are long, the money's not real flash, and it can prove dangerous with some of the ratbags and nutters out there. Furthermore, I admit that my navigational skills aren't particularly good.

It's an admission that I wish some cabbies would make. On more than one occasion I've had a street directory tossed to me by a driver as we hurtled along a freeway in a city I'm not familiar with, been asked to find where we're going, and then been irritated to discover we've been going in the wrong direction.

The worst was a little Burmese driver at Sydney airport. There were three of us who'd just come in on the overnight flight from Perth. We were dead on our feet, virtually fell into the cab, mumbled the address we wanted, and started to drowse just about as soon as we hit the seats.

An unknown number of minutes later I came to with a start. Maybe the snores of the two in the back seat woke me. I looked around blearily and thought 'This doesn't look right'.

Not right indeed. Somehow the idiot at the wheel had managed to get lost trying to get out of the airport. We were on one of the runways used by light planes. The big clue for me was the aircraft hangar we were going past.

"Where the hell are we?" I demanded.

"I not know!" said the idiot. "This first day on job for me. You all sleep. I not sure where to go."

We pulled over to the hangar, and when I could get the blokes working there to stop laughing I got directions for the way back out onto a useful road.

When we got to the road I said "Right, now pull over and we'll have a look at the map so you know where you're going."

"Okay," he said, and stopped at the side of the road.

As I opened the street directory I said, "You can take that meter back to zero now, too."

The driver started to wave his hands. "No do that! First day on job! No turn off meter!"

"You don't reckon we're gonna pay…" I squinted at the numbers, "… fifteen dollars to go round in circles, do you?"

"No can turn off meter!"

"Yes you bloody well can. Would you like me to ring up and explain this to your boss? Your first day on the job could be your last if you like."

With great reluctance he turned the meter off, starting it again from scratch as we pulled out onto the highway. Funnily enough I <u>didn't</u> go back to sleep again before we got to our destination.

*

I got caught another time on one of my first trips to Melbourne. As I entered the cab at the airport that night I told the guy the address I wanted – 265 something-or-other road.

"What suburb?" he asked in a strange Eastern European accent. When I told him he asked, "Where that? I not know there."

"That makes two of us, pal," I replied.

"I think I know where road is," he said, none too comfortingly, and we took off along the freeway. After a while we saw a turnoff sign indicating the suburb we were aiming for, among others. A bit later another of the big green direction signs told us that we'd inadvertently stumbled onto the road we were looking for.

Soon after that we spotted the number 275 on a shop front. The cab pulled over and the driver said "This close enough. You get out now. I in hurry."

I looked around and couldn't see the hotel I was supposed to be at. Over my protests he practically jettisoned me from the cab, accepting less than the metered fare just to get me out quickly before speeding away.

I looked at the row of closed shops. A school on the next block, a warehouse and vacant lots across the road didn't fill me with optimism. I dug out of my pocket the phone number of the hotel I wanted – damned glad I'd had enough sense to write it down when I booked, and rang them on my mobile.

I explained that I was standing outside 275 something-or-other road – where was the hotel?

"You should be able to see it half a block away," I was told. "Across from the railway station, near the burger bar."

"What burger bar? For that matter, what railway station?" I asked.

Further confused conversation followed.

At this point, I should explain something about Melbourne for those who've never been there. Particularly those from Brisbane.

Brisbane is, I think, the only state capital in Australia which really is only one city. One big metropolitan municipality with one council in charge. Melbourne and the others aren't. They're made up of lots of council areas, each calling themselves "cities" even if they only seem to be a few suburbs, or even blocks, in size.

The curious thing about Melbourne is that every time a road or street crosses a boundary between a couple of these little "cities" the property numbering starts again. So there could be several '275 something-or-other roads'. Worse perhaps if I'd been looking for a smaller number!

Having established that I was a long way from my destination, I tried to phone for another cab. To my puzzlement I couldn't get through to any of the taxi companies. Over an hour and a half's walk later, I finally found my hotel. All the way along the road I'd hoped to flag down a passing cab, but there wasn't a single one to be seen.

It was only when I was propped at the bar of my new digs, enjoying a much needed restorative ale, that I found out the story. It explained why my cabbie had been in such a hurry to ditch me and get away – there'd been a stop work and mass meeting of all Melbourne's taxi drivers called. The reason? To protest at state government proposals to improve service standards in the taxi industry.

*

For all that I've had a few rotten experiences, I must admit I've had a lot more cab journeys that haven't gone wrong. The great majority of drivers I've met have at least been pretty good, and several have been excellent.

I had one driver tell me the story of an aggravating bastard customer he'd had recently – a bank manager who regularly traveled by cab.

On their way across town the bankie started complaining about the number of cars overtaking them. "Keep up with the traffic! I'm in a hurry!" he demanded..

The driver ignored him and kept going as he was. Another couple of cars passed.

"I said keep up with the traffic!" shouted the passenger, and threw in a few choice descriptions of slow drivers.

"I'm doing the speed limit, and that's all I'm doing," explained the cabbie.

"That's not good enough. Keep up with the traffic – go faster!" was the reply, peppered with a bit more abuse.

The cabbie pulled over to the side of the motorway they were on. "If I get booked for speeding, I'm bloody sure you're not going to reach into yer pocket and pay my fine, are you? And even if ya did, it won't give me back the points on my licence. Now listen, I don't come into your office and tell you how to do whatever it is you do to people. Don't you bloody well sit there in my cab and tell me how to do my job."

"If ya don't like it," he continued, "I'm happy for ya to pay what's on the meter now, get out here, and take your chances flagging down another cab – one with a driver who doesn't give a bugger about whether he drives legally or safely."

The bank manager sank into his seat and muttered an apology, then the journey continued in silence.

A few weeks later, the same driver happened to pick up the same bank manager, who got into the cab without looking at who was behind the wheel. Soon after, they were overtaken and the bank manager started to exclaim "Keep up with the…" Just then he recognized who was driving. "Oh," he said sheepishly, "I'd better not say that to you."

The cabbie sighed. "Ya know, I'd really hoped you'd learned not to say it to *any* of us."

*

A mate of mine, Syd, is an office manager in town. He was having a problem with one of the women in his team, let's call her Sylvia.

Sylvia had a voice that cut the air like a machete. She spent a lot of time making private phone calls, which *everyone* in the office could hear. Several times Syd asked her to either keep it down or leave the room, to no avail.

Eventually he quietly called a few of the other staff together and asked them to keep diaries of what they heard.

After a month he called Sylvia into his office to again 'have a word' with her about her loud private phone calls. Sylvia indignantly insisted that she'd been the soul of discretion and Syd was obviously exaggerating.

Syd then presented a list of what she'd said, for how long and to whom. It even included details of her house sale, the new places she'd looked at buying, and all of the haggling that had been going on.

Maybe not the most conventional management practice in the world, but it worked. Sylvia learned to be quiet.

*

You don't need to be the sharpest knife in the drawer to work in television, anywhere in the world.

I was watching one of those music video clip shows back in 2010. Actually I couldn't find the remote control and was too tired to get out of the chair to change channels.

The host was a young bloke whose main talent seemed to be to the ability to talk at speed without inhaling.

He was enthusing about a clip by someone called 'Young MC'.

"Not so young any more," quipped the host. "He was born in 1967 so that makes him... um... 69 or something, doesn't it?"

I'll let you do the maths.

*

The furthest north point of Britain is the delightfully named Muckle Flugga, at the tip of the island of Unst. The only buildings up there are the lighthouse and the old RAF radar base.

The base is decommissioned now – mothballed rather than bulldozed I'm happy to say, but during the height of the Cold War it was an important installation.

As the Cold War wound down, though, things got a bit lax. The prospects of a flight of Russian bombers passing over the top end of the Shetlands seemed pretty remote. The blokes 'on duty' watching the radar screens would apparently spent a fair percentage of their shift with their feet up, enjoying a cup of tea and a read of the papers.

(This story comes from a local who was told it by one of the RAF boys working there, so *I'm* not calling their work into question, ok?)

One day the boys were momentarily distracted by a noise from the radar instrumentation. Alarmed, they checked the screen, but there was nothing to be seen. After some head scratching they returned to their tea and reading matter.

Minutes later, the noise was repeated. Again, a frantic scramble, but again, nothing on the screen.

The boys settle back into their chairs, but now they're keeping a wary eye out. Sure enough, a couple of minutes later the same thing happens, but with one key difference.

There's an almighty BOOM outside. The whole island of Unst shook, or at least everyone on the island heard the sound.

Of course, there was much consternation around the RAF base. Then the telex machine chattered into life. There was a one word message from a US Air Force base in northern Europe.

"Stealth".

The new stealth bomber was being tested. When the first two 'fly-past' efforts hadn't gotten a reaction the pilot apparently decided to make his presence known. The boom was the sound barrier being shattered, together with the equilibrium of that day's radar shift (not to mention the peace of mind of a lot of Unst residents)!

*

You don't have to come from a farming background to know what a scarecrow is. It's a thing stuck in a field to scare off crows that would otherwise damage the crop.

In several parts of Scotland, the crows are less of a problem than geese.

They flock in hundreds, or even thousands. The migratory ones are unpopular with many farmers, but thanks to the efforts of the Royal Society for the Preservation of Birds (an organization I'm impressed enough with to be a proud card-carrying member) there's actually a compensation payment available. Don't shoot the birds and you get some money to make up for the damage they do.

The damage is quite considerable. Geese are big eaters. They're also big birds – what they don't eat they tend to flatten, by weight as much as weight of numbers!

Migratory birds tend to be a bit skittish, and can be frightened off by an irate farmer – for a while at least. The 'resident' flocks however, seem to have gotten quite used to humans over the years. But what they apparently *have* learned to be very wary of is motor vehicles.

As you travel around rural Scotland you may think that the locals are really rotten drivers. In a lot of fields you'll spot wrecked or derelict cars, trucks or vans. The modern version of scarecrows – they're goose-frighteners.

*

Whatever job you do, you probably have noticed that when you get together with other people in the same industry you tend to 'talk shop'. Very especially, you tend to swap horror stories and funny stories – and particularly those stories that fall into both categories.

Hospital wardsmen are no exception.

In my experience, and I've checked this with others who've held the job in other parts of the world, the recurring topic of conversation when wardsmen gather is anal insertions.

The catalogue is long and, to me at least, eye-watering. Among the wide range of articles extracted, sometimes surgically (and sometimes with the aid of anaesthesia) the stand-outs are:

- cans of hairspray (and I use the plural deliberately)

- light bulbs

- a fluorescent tube

- half a milk bottle (the other half is best not thought about, I fear)

- a bicycle inner tube that had been cut and had a knot tied in the end.

The stories that accompany the items are the real imagination-stretchers. Variations on the theme of "I was changing the light fitting in my bathrobe and slipped…"

*

I was visiting a very posh Men's room in a very, very posh Sydney shop.

The place was so posh that the toilet had it's own concierge at the door. Not a scruffy old guy down on his luck – this dude was well turned out in a Store Uniform, slicked hair and shiny shoes.

To my intrigue though, on the floor of my otherwise immaculate cubicle I found a little plastic tray that still held a fork, some olive seeds and a few leftover black olives.

When I'd finished what I came for I took my discovery to the concierge.

"Is the floor here so clean you can eat off it?" I asked.

With barely a smile he replied, "We'd like to think so, sir, but we make the plates available just in case."

A man very good at his job, I reckon.

*

I'm always impressed by people who overcome adversity to achieve the stuff they really want to do.
Economic, social, psychological or physical adversity.

That last one used to be called 'disability' or more recently, being 'differently abled'.

I was chatting to a bloke recently who works for a really big Information Technology company based in Europe. With enormous respect in his voice he told me about a small group of programmers in his company.

The distinguishing feature of this group is that they're all blind.

Think about that for a moment. Blind computer programmers – they have Braille keyboards but can't see any monitor screens. As my mate explained, they retain the equivalent of whole screens full of coding (the raw data of programming) in their heads.

I wonder if they're able to do it because they don't have the distraction of a lot of visual information cluttering up their memories?

.o0o.

NO BASTARD IN PARTICULAR

I admit I'm a mark for funny car stickers. There are a lot of rubbish ones out there, but I've seen a few that I've really enjoyed.

A beat up old van parked at The Rocks in Sydney gave me a laugh with a sticker that asked:
"If 4 out of 5 people suffer from diarrhea, does that mean the 5th enjoys it?"

Sometimes it's a matter of circumstance – right place, right time, right person. For example, an old bastard I know in South Australia is what we might call a rather self-opinionated driver. I've seen a sticker that sums up his attitude perfectly:
"Why am I the only person on the planet who can drive?"

*

Jason, Paul, Wayne and I were sitting around having several drinks and letting the alcohol grease the creative gears of our brains. Conversation got around to teeny tiny little mobile phones that do a thousand things but have buttons so small you have to poke them with a plastic toothpick.

"Someone should invent a mobile phone just for blokes," observed Jason.

So over the next hour or two the concept of *The Blone* was explored.

The first obvious design element was that it would have big buttons to suit blokes' hands – even the ones with sausage fingers.

The default ring tone would be the 'Wide World Of Sports' theme, and it would be hardwired to prevent any 'chick songs' being downloaded to replace it.

The *Blone* would also have a special 'heads up' tone. This would sound whenever the bloke's wife/girlfriend was calling, or if she unexpectedly came into close proximity.

There was some debate about the look of the thing. The colours of your favourite footy team was a popular option. But there was also an argument for the reliable, easy to find safety colours of yellow and black.

A textured non-slip case seemed like a good idea, but it also had to be water resistant. After all, it wouldn't be the first time a phone fell into an esky.

Finally, this safety coloured, non-slip, water resistant case should be made of thick durable rubber. Because the *Blone* would still be a mobile phone and sometimes you do just want to throw the bloody thing across the room.

*

I should confess that I'm a bit of a collector of t-shirts. Several years ago Gill convinced me to have a bit of a cull when she did a rough count of the contents of several shelves full that I'd accumulated. She realized I had enough to wear a different t-shirt every day for well over a year.

My suggestion that surely this would save on laundry didn't help.

Since then the count has gone back up. I reckon I'm good for a couple of years now.

But all my shirts are obtained for a reason. I like their look, I think they're funny, or they commemorate something I've been involved in or enjoyed. Concert memorabilia, or souvenirs of places I've been.

I always figured that was most people's approach to t-shirt buying. Maybe I'm wrong. Or maybe some people have a sense of humour that's different to mine.

I don't find myself chuckling when I read the chest of some surly-looking bastard whose shirt informs me "I'm not ignoring you – I just don't give a f*ck about you". Well, you may be pleased to know that the feeling is mutual, pal.

*

I can always appreciate bastards who can laugh at themselves. I hope the bloke I saw walking down a street in Sydney was kidding.

He was, fair dinkum, one of the most unattractive individuals I've ever seen. He had a pot belly, skinny legs, rotten teeth, greasy hair, a lunar complexion and stubble that grew in patches like crab grass.

As he shuffled along, hands buried deep in the pockets of stained baggy shorts, I was intrigued by his t-shirt.

The artwork looked like two big ribbons and a bow, with the wrapping paper effect enhanced by a big tag on which was written *To: Women From: God*.

I reckon the Returns Counter would be busy.

*

Beauticians don't make a lot of money out of me. I'm first to admit I'm probably a lost cause, or at least a better candidate for a panel beater than a make-up artist.

But I've been known to buy skin care products for other people. Not because I think they need them, I hasten to add, but I'm happy to pamper someone I love.

I was walking home from a shopping trip carrying a couple of plastic bags from various stores. As I put them down I noticed that my fingers and palm were black. I was only carrying one black bag, and sure enough I could see where the colour had come off it all over my hand.

The irony was that it was the bag I'd gotten from the beauticians' shop, advertising – and containing – an expensive brand of skin cleanser.

I'd like to report that the product did a great job of removing the ink. Sadly it didn't. That was a job for hot water, heavy duty soap and a scrubbing brush.

*

As you might have noticed from this book's cover art, I have a beard. I have done for rather a lot of years now, regardless of whether it's fashionable or not.

For one thing, I think it's a kindness to sensitive souls to cover up at least some of my dial.

For another, I went to a school that absolutely INSISTED that the boys had to start shaving at the very first indication of any hint of fluff breaking the surface of the skin. The same autocratic insistence on hair being kept above the collar and the top of the ears explains why I've been largely a stranger to haircuts since the last day of final term.

Every so often, though, the facial hair has its down side. (*Down* side – get it? Never mind.)

I was staying overnight in a little place on the Queensland central coast. It was the very beginning of summer. After a couple of weeks of rain it was, at last, a hot fine day.

I turned on the little air conditioning unit. Nothing happened.

Peering close to the machine (not my brightest move, in hindsight, like looking down the barrel of a gun to see if its loaded) I gave it a minute or two. There was a strange rattling noise, then something like a pop from somewhere inside the unit.

The air blasted out in a rush, but it wasn't just air.

A colony of some sort of small black insect had made their spring home in some deep damp part of the inner workings.

A cloud of wet, irritated tiny bugs belched from the air conditioner fair into my face.

If I'd been clean-shaven, the task of washing them off would have been fairly straightforward. What was, at that point, a pretty full-on bushy beard gave the little buggers somewhere new to nest.

It took days of repeated shampooing to get rid of the last of them. Dog wash was starting to look tempting…

*

The thing about public transport is that you get to see stuff that might otherwise be discreetly hidden away as people travelled in the privacy of their own vehicle.

A bloke got onto a bus I was riding one morning recently. He was wearing a reasonably conservative shirt, but it wasn't tucked into his trousers. And it was a long enough shirt that this couldn't be accidental – this was a deliberate fashion statement. You can decide what the statement was.

His trousers were similarly conservative – lower/middle management office wear I suppose, an impression enhanced by the plain dark blue tie.

He was clean-shaven, well, if you allow for a blunt razor, while his hair was swept back in a ponytail that had caught maybe 80% of the hair intended for it. The rest just sort of hung or flopped about.

To complete his ensemble, on his feet was as ratty a pair of thongs as I've seen this side of the ones that get abandoned on beaches all over the world. And tucked under his arm, instead of a briefcase or the morning newspaper, was a well-worn skateboard.

I wondered where he'd come from and where he was going. Certainly, it was a case of mixed messages!

Another time, I was sitting on a Sydney train opposite a woman with teeth that made the Pogues' Shane McGowan look like Donny Osmond. Imagine a row of very old, weather-beaten gravestones.

Now, I appreciate that dental work in Australia doesn't come cheap, and even the best private medical insurance comes up pretty short.

But this woman was wearing ostentatious designer sunglasses, carrying an equally extravagant handbag, and waxing loud and lyrical on her mobile phone about the luxury unit she was renting. (In Sydney, that *must* have been pricey!)

So really, I think she could have afforded to invest a few quid in a mouth that wouldn't frighten children and farm animals.

*

I don't know about you, but I've wondered on several occasions about the phrase "the best thing since sliced bread". I mean, sliced bread is a great idea, but I pondered to myself, what was the best thing *before* sliced bread?

By happy chance, I have an answer. It turns out that in July of 1928, in the small US town of Chillicothe, Missouri was home to the birth of the Rohwedder Bread Slicer.

The local paper – the *Constitution Tribune* – was mightily enthused by the new invention. The entire front page was given over to serious coverage of the Bread Slicer, and the back page was completely filled by an ad for it. It was only an eight page publication, so a full quarter of its content that issue was bread-related!

It was positive but thoughtful editorial comment, too.

"The idea of sliced bread may be startling to some people… (but this) is a sound, sensible and in every way a progressive refinement in bakers' bread service. The slices stack perfectly, they are ideal for the making of neat, dainty sandwiches. For toasting purposes they are unexcelled."

As I read further I found an answer to the question I posed earlier. The editor of the *Constitution Tribune* glowingly described the new sliced loaf as "the greatest forward step in the baking industry since bread was wrapped."

So there you have it. Prior to 1928 you would have hoped your great new idea was the best thing since *wrapped* bread.

Maybe the bread industry has always held a special resonance for benchmark setters. There were more loaves than fishes when Jesus fed the multitude, according to the Bible story. Perhaps long ago nifty new things were considered the best thing since milled flour.

Ah well – such is loaf.

*

I wouldn't describe myself as a superstitious old bastard, but I do agree with Hamlet's observation that there are more things in heaven and earth than are dreamt of in your philosophy, Horatio.

I've had too many weird "coincidences" in my life to dismiss them all as mere random chance. This isn't the where or when to be talking about my own philosophy, I just wanted to make the point that for whatever reasons, strange things do happen. And they make good stories. I reckon that a greater proportion of 'urban myths' have their origins in true stories than those born from flights of fancy. There's a lot to be said for the old cliché about truth being stranger than fiction.

Now I know some of you will be shaking your heads about now. There are plenty of people who dismiss the whole idea of anything supernatural – until they hit their own threshold of things they can't explain.

Down in Tasmania there's a little place called Sarah Island. In years gone by it was home to a lot of convicts, but the settlement is long since abandoned. Nowadays tourists visit the ruined buildings, although not in the same numbers as go to some of the better known sites.

Like many such places it has its fair share of ghost stories. Visitors are told stories of the place being haunted or cursed by the former inmates. They're also told not to souvenir anything as it's a heritage site.

Not everyone takes either telling seriously, of course, but perhaps they should.

A tour guide from down that way told me about an English tourist who pinched half a brick from one of the ruined buildings and took it back home with him. Got away with it, too – nobody noticed it had gone.

The first anyone knew of it was a couple of months later when the half brick arrived in a parcel from London, addressed to the National Parks & Wildlife Service.

The enclosed note explained that the Englishman had had the most incredible run of bad luck ever since he left Sarah Island. Coincidence or curse, he wasn't taking any chances and provided very detailed instructions as to exactly where the half brick should be replaced.

I wonder whether the poor old bastard's luck improved.

*

I know an American lass named Delilah who reckons that there's a logical explanation for just about everything. Just about – she tells of one experience she's never been able to rationally and comfortably explain.

Delilah's Dad died when she was less than a year old. She wasn't taken to the funeral, and right throughout her childhood she was never taken to his gravesite, or even told where it was. Maybe her parents had fallen out, or maybe it was too painful for her mother for a long while.

When Delilah was about twelve she went with her Mum and a friend to a Memorial Day service at one of the big cemeteries in the large city that was their home.

After the service, while her mother and friend were standing around chatting to people, Delilah wandered off to look at headstones. I guess it's the natural curiosity of an intelligent twelve-year-old.

Delilah reckons "There was this one grave off by itself that seemed to call to me, yet at the same time it scared the begeesus out of me. It had no headstone, just a little metal marker."

As she'd done at several similar spots, Delilah went to bend down and read the marker. But as she went to do so she got this really strong nasty knot in her stomach and had to move away. Then when she did, the spot seemed to call her back to try again to read the marker.

This happened several times before a very shaken Delilah gave up and went back to her mother and friend.

Her Mum asked if "since we're here anyway" did she want to see her father's grave? Bear in mind, this was the first time Delilah even knew it was the cemetery he was buried in.

Sure enough, they started heading towards the 'calling grave'.

Delilah stopped dead in her tracks. When her Mum asked what was wrong Delilah just pointed and asked, "Is it that one?"

"Yes. What's wrong?" asked her mother.

Delilah explained what had been happening. Her mother reckoned she'd gone as pale as a sheet.

"It was the only contact I ever remember having with my Dad, and it wasn't pleasant!" said Delilah.

*

English is a funny old language. A lot of it doesn't sound the way it's spelt, and isn't spelt the way it sounds. Or there are multiple ways of spelling the same sound, which may then have different meanings.

Ern is an old mate who studied English at Uni years ago, and has retained a fascination for words ever since. He put together the following verses a while back, and while they look like gibberish at first glance I reckon they're worth recounting.

> A strain soil lettuce read Joyce four weir yunnan flea
> Weave gull danes oil in welfare awl aromas gert buy see
> Owl lands up pounds innate your skiffs off boot ear itchin' rear
> Inn hiss trees pay Gillette avarice stay judge vans astray yer fare
> Injure fools trains den lettuce sink add vans astray yer fare.
>
> Bean either rage dunce are think Ross wield oil weave art sand dance
> Tomb eighth is Carmen well far vows wren noun dove author lance
> Fourth owes hoove calm ark Ross these seize weave bounder lisp lanes twos yeah
> Weave car edge lettuce awl come bind ooh add vans astray lure fare
> Inn jaw fools drains thin lettuce inn add vans astray lure fare.

If you can't make heads or tails of any of that, try reading it with the tune of the Aussie national anthem in your head

For those who weren't even aware that *Advance Australia Fair* has more than one verse, the original words to the second go like this.

> Beneath our radiant Southern Cross we'll toil with heart and hands
> To make this Commonwealth of ours renowned of all the lands
> For those who've come across the seas we've boundless plains to share
> With courage all let us combine to advance Australia fair
> In joyful strains then let us sing advance Australia fair.

It takes a special kind of mind to come up with an effort like Ern's – thanks mate.

.o0o.

THE LAST WORD

The logo for *Gill's Old Bastards* includes a stylized angel, representing Gill's role in the formation of the group.

Personally, I believe that there really are guardian spirits, or angels, who will look after all of us if we let them. If you don't happen to agree that's okay, but it works for me.

A mother and her daughter were sitting together on a park bench. The kid pointed up into the clouds and said excitedly, "Look Mum! Angels!"

A miserable old bastard walking past grumbled to the bloke beside him, "How sad is that? Seeing angels where there's nothing but clouds."

I reckon it's a lot sadder to see nothing but clouds where there are angels.

I think angels look after people in lots of ways – oftentimes using other people as 'agents' (whether those people actually realize it or not). The helping hand you give someone may be their angel's way of sorting out a problem.

Just because you're an Old Bastard doesn't mean you can't be, shouldn't be, or aren't already, somebody's angel.

Cheers.

Renoir

You too can be one of Gill's Old Bastards!

GOBs MEMBERSHIP APPLICATION FORM

The Rules (such as they are) :

1. Marital status of parents is irrelevant. See Rule 2.
2. Age is irrelevant - it is sufficient to have been acclaimed at least once by friends as an Old Bastard.
3. Drinking habits must be hearty and jovial, whatever the drink of choice.
4. On encountering other OB's one must administer a hearty slap on the back, together with the cheerful greeting "Hello, you Old Bastard!"
5. Membership card or badge must be carried at all times. Failure to produce same when challenged by another OB incurs a penalty of one round of drinks.

If you feel you can live up to these conditions and be known as a good Old Bastard we'd love you to join us. $15 will get you Life Membership, a personalised card and a keyring badge.

Please complete and post with Membership fee to

AOOB   PO Box 2686   Southport Q 4215   OR

e-mail to gillsoldbastards@gmail.com with advice on how you'll be paying your fee
(* bank transfers can be made to: Acc name: AOOB – Brisbane
Acc number: 237033   BSB number: 034-003)
(Please include your surname and MEMB in the Description line – thanks.)

NAME: Mr/Mrs./Ms/ ....

ADDRESS: ....

.... Postcode: ....

E-MAIL: ....

NOMINATED BY: **#334752** *Renoir* SECONDED BY: **#346725** *P K Tate*

Thanks – and welcome!

www.ingramcontent.com/pod-product-compliance
Lightning Source LLC
Chambersburg PA
CBHW021128300426
44113CB00006B/340